The Escape of
Bonnie Prince
Charlie

Malcolm Seddon

Spiderwize
Remus House
Coltsfoot Drive
Woodston
Peterborough PE2 9BF

www.spiderwize.com

A CIP catalogue record for this book is available from
the British Library.

The views expressed in this work are solely those of the
author and do not necessarily reflect the views of the
publisher, and the publisher hereby disclaims any
responsibility for them.

Graphics and book design: Richard Johnson
Illustrations: Paul Osborne

ISBN: 978-1-911113-65-2

To my wife, Susan

Contents

INTRODUCTION TO THE HILLWALKERS' GUIDE

The best way to appreciate the landscape and locations that figure in this story is to follow Charles' actual routes, and visit the key places. The details are described in the *Hillwalkers' Guide*, which can be accessed free of charge on a dedicated website.

www.bpcbooks.co.uk

The *Hillwalkers' Guide* describes the routes as a sequence of individual walks, each lasting a few hours to a whole day. The detailed itinerary of each walk can be read on screen, or stored on a computer, etc. It can be printed as a pdf document. The *Hillwalkers' Guide*, together with Ordnance Survey maps, may also be useful in reading some parts of the story.

'For a prince to be a-skulking five long months exposed to the hardships of hunger and cold, thirst and nakedness, and surrounded on all hands by a numerous army of blood-thirsty men, both by sea and land, eagerly hunting after the price of blood, and yet that they should miss the much coveted aim, is an event of life far surpassing the power of words to paint'

Bishop Robert Forbes,
The Lyon in Mourning

Map showing Charles' total movements, 16 April - 20 September, 1746.

9

1
SETTING THE SCENE

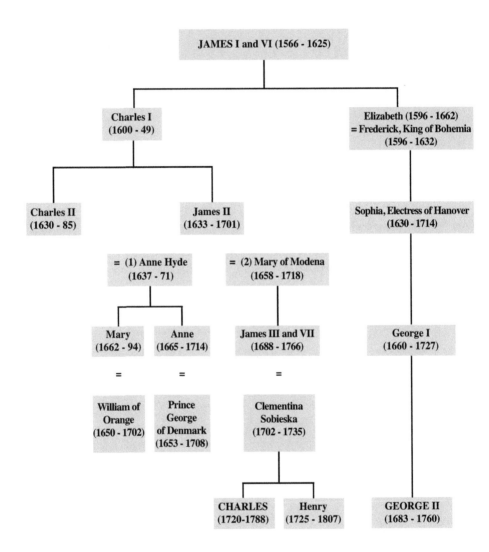

Family tree showing the descendents of James I and VI

The Background

On 10 June, 1688, the second wife of King James II gave birth to a son, who automatically became the heir to the thrones of England and Scotland. As James was a Roman Catholic convert, the Protestants feared that this birth would lead to a Roman Catholic dynasty. They therefore brought about the 'Glorious Revolution', in which James was deposed. He fled to France on 11 December, 1688.

For the Protestants, the only acceptable successors among James' children were the two Protestant daughters born to his first wife. Consequently, the succession went to the elder daughter, Mary, who ruled jointly with her husband, William of Orange.

Although James' deposition had had popular support, he had allies remaining in Britain. These 'Jacobites' were strongest in the Catholic areas of Ireland and Scotland. In 1689, James rallied the Irish Jacobites in an attempt at counter-revolution. However, he was finally defeated at the Battle of the Boyne a year later. James spent the rest of his life in France. On his death in 1701, the Jacobites transferred their allegiance to James Edward, the son whose birth had precipitated the crisis in 1688.

After the deaths of William and Mary, James' younger daughter, Anne, reigned from 1702 to 1714. As she died without leaving any living children, the crown left the House of Stewart for the House of Hanover. It went to George I, who, like James, was a great-grandson of James I, but in a different line of descent. On his death in 1727, the crown went to his son, George II.

From his residence in Rome, James took on his father's mantle of trying to regain the British throne. In 1708, he persuaded the French to help him invade Scotland. However, the fleet was dispersed by the Royal Navy before any troops landed. One year after the Hanoverian succession,

he instigated a rebellion in Lancashire and Scotland, but by February, 1716, it had petered out. In 1719, he tried again with Spanish mercenaries landing at Loch Duich in Wester Ross. After only a few days, this force was defeated in a brief skirmish at Glen Shiel, just six miles inland. On returning to Rome, James immediately married the Polish princess, Clementina Sobieska. On New Year's Day, 1720, she gave birth to Charles Edward Louis John Casimir Silvester Severino Maria. This was 'Bonnie Prince Charlie'.

From that point, James and his family were under permanent surveillance by Hanoverian spies. Nevertheless, James maintained contact with the British Jacobites through secret correspondence. James knew very well that, if he were to make another attempt, he would need Britain's other European enemies to support him. As before, his most obvious ally was France, where Louis XV made no secret of his desire to invade England. James had two agents permanently in Paris to keep open the channels of communication.

Back in Scotland, the Hanoverians took steps to prevent any more rebellions. In 1724, General Wade proposed the construction of forts to be used as bases for Independent Companies of Highland troops, loyal to the Hanoverian government. By 1740, he had completed Fort William, Fort Augustus and Fort George in the Great Glen, as well as Ruthven barracks at Kingussie. These military strongholds were connected to each other and to the south by a system of roads. One road ran the whole length of the Great Glen. Another climbed over the Corrieyairack Pass from Fort Augustus to Ruthven.

Despite these repressive measures, the Highland Jacobites remained active.

Furthermore, as the Hanoverian government became increasingly unpopular, the Jacobites grew in strength. In 1737, a mission of prominent Highland chiefs travelled to Rome, and informed James that many clans were ready to rise on his behalf. They urged him to mount another invasion.

'Therefore in ye nem of God let it please your Majestie to consider the present Juncture and that tyme and opportunitie is not to be neglected.'

James assured them of his resolve to renew the campaign in the near future. The mission therefore returned to Scotland, where a Jacobite Association was set up to make preparations.

Once Charles was in his twenties, it was obvious that he, rather than his father, would lead the invasion. Moreover, the 'Young Pretender' was eager to have a go. The opportunity arrived in December, 1743, when Louis XV, decided to take advantage of a general war in Europe to invade England. When he informed James of his intention, Charles immediately made his way to Paris.

In March, 1744, the invasion was aborted, when two storms devastated the French fleet in the Channel. Despite this fiasco, Louis formally declared war on Britain, but prevaricated about preparing another invasion. For months, the only visible sign of war was a blockade of the French Channel ports by the British navy.

In August, 1744, Murray of Broughton, a member of the mission to Rome in 1737, visited Charles in Paris, and revealed that the Highland clans would raise 4,000 men, provided Charles brought a French army. Charles replied that he was determined to come to Scotland, 'if he brought only a single footman'.

Exasperated with Louis' dithering, Charles now decided to 'go it alone'. With a few friends, he made secret plans to take arms and mercenaries to the West Highlands. From the information he had received, he was confident that he would immediately muster the Camerons, MacPhersons, MacGregors, Appin Stewarts, and MacLeods, together with the MacDonalds of Sleat, Glengarry, Glencoe and Clanranald. He hoped that, once other clans realised the strength of his support, they would also join the invasion of England. There, he hoped to rally the English Jacobites as well, and drive George II from London.

Charles sent a message conveying his intentions to the Highland chiefs, and raised money from a group of very rich emigré Jacobites. One of them, Antoine Walsh, masterminded the whole enterprise, and provided a 16-gun privateer frigate, *La du Teillay*. Another Jacobite, Walter Ruttledge, hired a 64-gun man-of-war, *Elisabeth*, together with 700 soldiers from an Irish regiment in the service of France. On 22 June, 1745, the expedition left St Nazaire with Charles and Walsh in *La du Teillay*.

Some days later, they enountered HMS *Lion* in the Atlantic. In the ensuing battle, the *Elisabeth* was so badly damaged that she was forced to return to France, taking most of the arms and all the troops with her. Despite this setback, Charles insisted on continuing to Scotland. On 23 July, he landed on the island of Eriskay. The very next day, he began contacting the chiefs who had already committed themselves to his cause.

The following story is about the relationships that developed. To understand what happened, it will be helpful to learn more about the Prince and the clans.

The Prince

Charles' early years were overshadowed by the bitter rift that separated his parents soon after he was five. For years, the couple lived apart. During this time, Charles and his younger brother, Henry, were brought up under the oppressive regime prescribed by his austere, ascetic father.

Although Charles became proficient in English, French, Spanish and Italian, he was not a good student. He was intelligent, but, much to his father's exasperation, Charles did not apply himself to his studies. Neither did he have much interest in religion. Henry, however, was a natural scholar. Despite being five years younger, than his brother, he eventually overtook Charles academically. Henry also became a very devout Catholic. As a consequence, Henry was James' favourite, while Charles had to suffer frequent shows of paternal disapproval.

In reaction, Charles became the archetypal rebellious child, clashing frequently with his father and other figures of authority. His attitude and behaviour were exacerbated by the influence of one his tutors, Sir Thomas Sheridan, who indulged the wilfulness and obstinacy of the student prince.

In contrast to his limited academic achievements, Charles showed a precocious aptitude for outdoor pursuits and social skills. At a very early age, he became expert in riding, hunting, shooting and golf. He also learned to dance, and play the cello very well. Despite the tensions and strife of his family life, Charles' public persona was mature and confident. Even as a teenager, his conversation was engaging, considerate and thoughtful. On formal occasions, his charismatic charm impressed everyone he met.

After the death of his mother in 1735, Charles gradually broke away from his father's repressive influence. He devoted himself almost entirely to hunting. Obsessed with achieving physical fitness, he continually sought the challenges of the most difficult terrain, and weather conditions. In this way, he developed great determination, drive, will-power, and self-confidence. Once in his twenties, this tall dashing young man with brown eyes, reddish hair and a delicate complexion was Prince Charming personified.

Prince Charles Edward Stuart

'But which shines most in him and renders him, without exception, the most surprisingly handsome person of the age, is the dignity which accompanies every gesture.'

The Clans

The clan system was based on the traditional belief that all members of one clan were descended from a common forebear. As a consequence, every member of the clan had the same surname. The names of clan chiefs and their lieutenants, - known as 'cadets' or 'tacksmen' - always included the name of a place. In practice, this place name was the sole means by which such a man was known. Ewan MacPherson of Cluny, was known simply as 'Cluny'. Aeneas MacDonald of Borrodale was just called 'Borrodale'. Although it is usually clear from the context whether a name refers to the place or a man, this book uses a simple typographical device to lessen the chance of confusion. When referring to places with names that include words such as 'Loch' or 'Glen', initial letters for the name of the loch or glen are printed in the upper case. The lower case is used when referring to people. Thus, Glen Aladale refers to the place, whereas Glenaladale refers to the man.

When a son of a chief or tacksman reached an age where he would begin to take a part in the chief's business, the epithets 'Young' and 'Old' were used to distinguish the two men. Old Clanranald was the chief. Young Clanranald was his son.

In practice, the great distances from London, and the lack of any roads, made it very difficult for the Hanoverian government to control the Highlands and Islands. The real power was in the hands of the chiefs. A chief could summon any of his clansmen to fight on the clan's behalf. Depending on the size of the clan, the chiefs could muster 200 - 2,500 men. Any clansman, who disobeyed this call, had the roof of his house set on fire.

Each chief let houses and land to his clansfolk. Rent was always paid in kind, such as oats, barley and cattle. Some clansmen, called 'boomen', worked with the chief in a profit-sharing arrangement.

The territories of some clans

Chief	Cadets
MacDonald of Clanranald	Boisdale
	Kinlochmoidart
	Glenaladale
	Morar
	Borrodale
	Milton
MacDonald of Sleat	Armadale
	Kingsburgh
	Baleshare
MacDonnell of Keppoch	Tiendrish
	Tullochrom
MacDonnell of Glengarry	Lochgarry
	Barrisdale
	Scotus

The principal clans of MacDonald and their cadets

In general, there was insufficient land for the needs of all the clansfolk. The land was always of very poor quality both for cultivating crops and grazing cattle. The difficulties were made even worse by the harsh weather that frequently destroyed or blighted harvests. After paying rent, clansfolk usually retained insufficient oats and barley to eat, let alone sell. Bread was available only in spring. The clansfolk therefore lived at starvation level on a diet of milk, whey, butter, and cheese. Common people rarely ate meat, but, in desperation, they would resort to drinking the blood of cattle.

Their houses were crude cottages or 'bothies'. Although the style and structure varied from place to place, they all had low stone walls, and turfed or thatched roofs, that leaked badly on to the bare earth floors. Many bothies had only a single dimly lit room, that might be shared with cattle. Often, the ceiling was too low for an adult to stand erect. An open peat fire in the middle of the floor filled the room with smoke, that eventually escaped through a hole in the roof. In summer, when the clansfolk took their cattle to remote grazing lands or 'shielings', they occupied even more primitive shiely huts, built from whatever materials could be found locally.

Being in receipt of rent from the common people, chiefs had more than sufficient to feed their families and entertain their guests. However, the geographical remoteness of their lands made it very difficult to sell their crops and cattle in the cities. As a consequence, most of the gentry were not rich in terms of cash.

A typical cottage reconstructed on Skye

15

Only a few chiefs, such as Cameron of Lochiel and MacPherson of Cluny, were sufficiently wealthy to have grand houses or castles. Many chiefs lived in houses only slightly superior to those of the common folk. Nevertheless, they would have four or five servants.

While the lowly folk spoke only Erse, the eighteenth century version of Gaelic, the gentry were well educated. They could speak English and French, and learned Latin and Greek at foreign universities.

The most common form of day-to-day dress for all classes was the plaid, or long tartan blanket. Men would wind one end round the waist as a kilt, and use the other as a shawl. Women would wear it wrapped loosely round the head and body. For common folk, the plaid was made of coarse homespun worsted.

Highland dress

The gentry had plaids of finer material. As alternatives, they wore more fashionable items made by travelling tailors. For example, men wore brightly coloured tight-fitting trews, waistcoats, and bonnets adorned with an eagle's feather. They also had short kilts or 'philibegs' worn with long stockings up to the knee. Ladies wore dresses.

Despite the wretchedness of their lot, the clansfolk, high and low, had an all-pervading sense of honour. The swearing of an oath on a drawn dirk made a commitment that could not be broken without incurring total disgrace. This underlying spirit was reflected in the strong bond of loyalty that the common people had to their chief. In their eyes, his main duty was to uphold and defend the honour of the clan.

A highland settlement

The Story

24 July- 5 December

Charles' first visitor on Eriskay was Alexander MacDonald of Boisdale, who came over from South Uist. Boisdale brought the news that the two mighty chiefs on Skye, Sir Alexander MacDonald of Sleat and the Laird of MacLeod, now refused to 'come out' because Charles had not brought any French troops.

> 'Every body was strock as with a thunder boult, as you may believe, to hear yt sentence.'

When Boisdale suggested that Charles should return home, Charles replied, 'I am come home, sir, and I will entertain no notion at all of returning to that place from whence I came; for I am persuaded my faithful Highlanders will stand by me.'

Undaunted, Charles sailed for the mainland, and, wearing Highland dress, disembarked with seven companions and just £4,000 at Loch nan Uamh* in Moidart. These 'Seven Men of Moidart' included the ageing Sir Thomas Sheridan, and Colonel John O'Sullivan, who was the military adviser.

Charles now summoned the local and more distant chiefs to join his cause. Initially, most of them were reluctant to do so. However, Charles persisted, and, using his charisma and charm, eventually convinced many that the French were likely to invade Britain, as soon as the clans were seen to be in serious revolt.

For a few days, the issue hung in the balance. Charles eventually recruited the Clanranald MacDonalds of Borrodale, Glen Aladale, Kinlochmoidart and Morar.

The various movements between 24 July and 5 December.

He was also joined by Young Clanranald, who in the dotage of his father, was the effective head of the Clanranald MacDonalds. Cameron of Lochiel ('Gentle Lochiel') - threw in his lot after Charles promised full security for the Cameron estates, that would certainly be forfeited, if the rebellion failed. Murray of Broughton became Charles' secretary.

* Pronunciation: lokh nan oo-av
  Translation: lake of caves'

On 4 August, Charles was confident enough to send Walsh back to France with the ship. Charles himself took up residence in Borrodale House, the home of Aeneas MacDonald. After raising his standard at Glen Finnan on 19 August, Charles began the march south with his embryo army of 1,700 men. In Badenoch, he recruited Ewan MacPherson of Cluny, who was an officer in the Hanoverian army. Cluny had to be kidnapped, and agreed to join the rebels only after being promised the same security already given to his cousin, Lochiel.

Loch nan Uamh near Borrodale

The Hanoverian government, having been aware of Charles' arrival for some time, offered a reward of £30,000 for his arrest. General Cope was sent with a force of raw recruits to destroy Charles' army. However, instead of joining battle at the Corrieyairack Pass on 28 August, Cope retreated to Inverness. One month later, Charles defeated Cope in a battle at Prestonpans, just east of Edinburgh. He then marched into Edinburgh, where, capitalising on his enthusiastic reception, he raised almost a whole regiment from the local population.

On learning of Charles' victory and capture of Edinburgh, more clans came down from the Highlands to join him. Even Sir Alexander MacDonald decided to send 900 men. However, he was blackmailed into changing his mind, when the Lord President, Duncan Forbes, threatened to expose him for deporting some clansfolk to the colonies.

Flushed with success, Charles now crossed the border. By the beginning of December, the army of 5,500 had reached Derby without meeting any opposition.

When news of Charles' progress reached France, Louis issued a formal proclamation of support. Louis also decided to invade the south coast of England. News of Louis' intentions was conveyed to Charles in England, and to James in Rome.

Immediately, Charles' brother, Henry, set off from Rome to take part in the invasion.

Royal proclamation offering a reward for Charles' capture

By the Lords Juſtices,

A PROCLAMATION;

Ordering a Reward of Thirty thouſand Pounds to any Perſon who ſhall ſeize and ſecure the Eldeſt Son of the Pretender, in caſe He ſhall land, or attempt to land, in any of His Majeſty's Dominions.

Jo. Cant.	Devonſhire,	Bedford,	Cheſterfield,
Hardwicke, C,	Grafton,	Holles Newcaſtle,	Stair,
Dorſet, P.	Bolton,	Tweeddale,	H. Pelham.
Gower, C. P. S.			

WHEREAS by an Act of Parliament made in the Seventeenth Year of His Majeſty's Reign, it was Enacted, That if the Eldeſt, or any other Son or Sons of the Perſon who preſumed to be Prince of Wales in the Life-time of the late King James the Second, and, ſince his Deceaſe, aſſumed the Name and Title of James the Third, King of England, Scotland, and Ireland, ſhould, after the Firſt Day of May, in the Year One thouſand ſeven hundred and forty four, land, or attempt to land, or be found in Great Britain or Ireland, or any of the Dominions or Territories belonging to the Crown of Great Britain, or ſhould be found on board any Ship, Veſſel, or Boat, being ſo on board with Intent to land in Great Britain or Ireland, or any of the Dominions or Territories aforeſaid, He and They reſpectively ſhould, by virtue of the ſaid Act, ſtand and be adjudged attainted of High Treaſon, to all Intents and Purpoſes whatſoever: And whereas We have received Information, that the Eldeſt Son of the ſaid Pretender did lately embark in France, in order to land in ſome Part of His Majeſty's Kingdoms, We being moved with juſt Indignation at ſo daring an Attempt, and deſirous that the ſaid Act may be carried effectually into Execution, have thought fit, by the Advice of His Majeſty's Privy Council, and do hereby, in His Majeſty's Name, command and require all His Majeſty's Officers, Civil and Military, and all other His Majeſty's loving Subjects, to uſe their utmoſt Endeavours to ſeize and ſecure the ſaid Son of the Pretender, whenever he ſhall land, or attempt to land, or be found in Great Britain or Ireland, or any of the Dominions or Territories belonging to the Crown of Great Britain, or ſhall be found on board any Ship, Veſſel, or Boat, being ſo on board with Intent to land in Great Britain or Ireland, or any of the Dominions or Territories aforeſaid, in order to His being brought to Juſtice, and to give Notice thereof immediately, when He ſhall be ſo ſeized and ſecured, to One of His Majeſty's Principal Secretaries of State: And to the Intent that all due Encouragement may be given to ſo important a Service, We do hereby further, in His Majeſty's Name, promiſe a Reward of Thirty thouſand Pounds, to ſuch Perſon and Perſons who ſhall ſo ſeize and ſecure the ſaid Son of the ſaid Pretender, ſo as that He may be brought to Juſtice: And His Majeſty's High Treaſurer, or the Commiſſioners of His Majeſty's Treaſury for the time being, is and are hereby required to make Payment thereof accordingly. And if any of the Perſons who have adhered to, or aſſiſted, or who ſhall adhere to, or aſſiſt the ſaid Pretender, or His ſaid Son, ſhall ſeize and ſecure him the ſaid Son, as aforeſaid; be it, that, who ſhall ſo ſeize and ſecure him, ſhall have His Majeſty's Gracious Pardon, and ſhall alſo receive the ſaid Reward, to be paid in Manner aforeſaid.

Given at *Whitehall*, the Firſt Day of *Auguſt*, in the Nineteenth Year of His Majeſty's Reign.

God ſave the King.

LONDON,

Printed by *Thomas Baskett*, Printer to the King's moſt Excellent Majeſty; and by the Aſſigns of *Robert Baskett*. M.DCC.XLV.

CHARLES
Prince of *Wales*, &c.

Regent of the Kingdoms of *Scotland*, *England*, *France* and *Ireland*, and the Dominions thereunto belonging.

WHEREAS We have seen a certain scandalous and malicious Paper, published in the Stile and Form of a Proclamation, bearing Date the 1st instant, wherein under Pretence of bringing Us to Justice, like Our Royal Ancestor King *Charles* the I. of blessed Memory, there is a Reward, of Thirty Thousand Pounds *Sterling*, promised to those who shall deliver Us into the Hands of Our Enemies : We could not but be moved with a just Indignation at so insolent an Attempt. And tho' from Our Nature and Principles We abhor and detest a Practice, so unusual among Christian Princes, We cannot but out of a just Regard to the Dignity of our Person, promise the like Reward of Thirty Thousand Pounds *Sterling*, to him or those who shall seize and secure, till Our further Orders, the Person of the Elector of *Hanover*, whether landed, or attempting to land, in any Part of His Majesty's Dominions. Should any fatal Accident happen from hence, let the Blame ly entirely at the Door of those who first set the infamous Example.

CHARLES, P. R.

Given in Our Camp at *Kinlocheill*,
  August the 22d, 1745.

By His Highness Command,

JO. MURRAY,

Charles' proclamation offering a reward for the capture of George II

5 December
- 16 April

Despite their success, the morale of many clan chiefs was very low. On the way from the border, Charles had recruited only a handful of English Jacobites. There was also a steady flow of deserters from his army. Intelligence agents were reporting that two Hanoverian armies, led by the Duke of Cumberland and General Wade, were closing from the east and west. In addition, there had been no news of the invasion by the French for over a month. In these circumstances, many clan chiefs did not want to march on to London. On 5 December, 'Black Friday', Charles' Grand Council decided to turn back from Derby towards Scotland. Charles was furious and deeply distressed.

The news of this retreat did not reach France until 18 December. Disappointed though he was, Louis did not stop his preparations for an invasion. However, the combined effects of adverse weather, and the blockade by the British fleet gradually persuaded him that the venture was too dangerous. The invasion was effectively abandoned in the first week of January.

With Charles' prospects looking increasingly gloomy, the thoughts of his friends in France turned to organising a rescue. Walsh now ordered the commanders of the supply ships to bring Charles back, if there had been some disastrous military reverse. Three expeditions set sail in March. Captain Rouillée and Captain Lory were in two men-of-war, *Le Mars* and *La Bellone*.

The various movements between 5 December and 16 April.

The other two were commanded respectively by François Dumont in the cutter, *Le Hardi Mendiant*, and Pierre Anguier in the brigantine, *Le Bien Trouvé*.

On the way north, Charles' army won a battle over Hanoverian forces at Falkirk, and scattered a small force of Lord Loudoun's troops at Moy. In March, Charles reached Inverness, where he could only wait for the inevitable confrontation with the Duke of Cumberland, whose army had been in steady pursuit. The battle took place at Culloden in the early afternoon of 16 April. After about half an hour, Charles' army was routed.

Duke of Cumberland

'Yu see, all is going to pot!'

Hanoverian soldiers

23

2
16 - 26 APRIL
CULLODEN to BORRODALE

The distraught Charles was led from the battlefield on horseback by Lord Elcho, Sir Thomas Sheridan, and Charles' aide-de-camp, Alexander MacLeod of Muiravonside. By pure chance, they met MacLeod's servant, Edward (Ned) Burke. With the protection of sixty dragoons from Fitz-James Horse, Burke guided them for four miles to the river Nairn, where they stopped.

Soon, they were joined by O'Sullivan, who had ridden after them from the battlefield.

Charles, now in a desperately paranoid state of mind, believed that he had been betrayed.

'He neither Spoke to any of the Scots officers present or inquired after any of the Absent..... He appeared very Uneasy as long as the Scots were about him.'

The various movements between 16 and 26 April

Fearing that the Scots might hand him over to the enemy, Charles dismissed most of the dragoons, and sent orders for the remnants of his army to gather at Ruthven in two days' time. However, Charles, himself, planned to ride to Fort Augustus, with Elcho, Sheridan, MacLeod, O'Sullivan, and an escort comprising the remaining few members of Fitz-James Horse.

As Burke knew the way very well, 'The Prince was pleased to say to Ned, if you be a true friend, pray endeavour to lead us safe off. Which honour Ned was not a little fond of, and promised to do his best.'

'Sir, if you please, follow me. I'll do my endeavour to make you safe.'

They rode by the river Nairn into the Great Glen. After some 20 miles, they stopped at Gortuleg, where the household had been preparing a feast to celebrate the anticipated Jacobite victory. Over three glasses of wine, Charles told the woeful news to Lord Lovat, who was staying at Gortuleg as a house guest. However, Lovat encouraged Charles to continue the fight. His words evidently lifted Charles' spirits. He instructed MacLeod to write a buoyant letter to Cluny, whose regiment had not reached Culloden in time for the battle. The letter ordered Cluny to bring his men to Fort Augustus the next day.

'D^r. Sir,
You have (heard) no doubt ere now of the ruffle we met with this forenoon. We have suffered a good deal; but hope we shall soon pay Cumberland in his own coin.
We are to review to-morrow at Fort Augustus the Frasers, Camerons, Stewart, Clanronalds, and Keppoch's people. His R.H. expects your People will be with us at Furthest Friday morning. Dispatch is the more necessary that his Highness has something in view which will make an ample amends for this day's ruffle.'

(16 April, 1746)

After a rest of two hours, Charles and his retinue set off down the Great Glen. Despite their original plans, they stopped only briefly at Fort Augustus, and rode on to Invergarry Castle, which they reached in the early hours of the morning.

The castle was deserted and 'without meat, fire or candle except some firr-sticks'. Fortunately, Ned Burke discovered a fishing net in the river, and, pulling it ashore, found two salmon which he 'made ready in the best manner he could, and the meat was reckoned very savoury and acceptable'. They spent the remainder of the night resting, and discussing what they should do next. Overnight, they were joined by Charles' confessor, Father Allan MacDonald, who had travelled from Culloden with some other fugitives from the battle.

None of Charles' friends was willing to advise him what to do next. Next morning, Charles made up his own mind.

'Well,' says the Prince, 'I see as well as yu yt my scituation is desperate, it is in those occasions where a man must take his party sooner then in any other.'

He then announced his intention to leave Scotland, sail to France, and return soon with a French army. At this decision, Lord Elcho left in disgust.

Charles' immediate destination, was the west coast at Arisaig, where he hoped to find a ship. With Ned Burke as guide, his plan was to take O'Sullivan and Father Macdonald. Sheridan, being too old to travel fast, had to follow with some other men. The dragoons were ordered back to Inverness. MacLeod was dispatched to Ruthven with a message of *sauve qui peut* for the remnants of Charles' army.

'Let every man seek his safety in the best way he can.'

At three o' clock in the afternoon, Charles, with his three companions, set off down the north-west shore of Loch Lochy. Before leaving, Charles put on Burke's coat in order not to be easily recognised. They started on horseback, but were eventually forced to make most of the way on foot.

The head of Loch Arkaig

At the southern end of Loch Lochy, they turned west towards Loch Arkaig. After a brief stop for refreshment at the home of Cameron of Clunes, Charles sent Burke to seek news at Achnacarry, the seat of Lochiel. However, nobody in the house knew anything apart from the result of the battle. They then rode on along the northern shore of the loch. Once again, the going was very difficult.

'In this road we had got ourselves all nastied.'

Round about midnight, they reached Kinlocharkaig, and found shelter in the house of Donald Cameron of Glen Pean. By this time, Charles, who had hardly slept for five days, was totally exhausted, and needed help to undress. During the process, seven guineas fell on the floor.

When Ned retrieved them, Charles said, 'Thou art a trusty friend and shall continue to be my servant.'

A ruined cottage at Kinlocharkaig

Throughout the next day, Charles remained at Kinlocharkaig, hoping to hear news from people who might have been coming behind him. Having heard nothing by five o'clock, he decided to continue towards the coast with Donald Cameron as guide. As the way down Glen Pean was unsuitable for horses, they set off on foot, sending the horses a different way.

Gleann a' Chaorainn from the head of Loch Arkaig

Glen Pean

27

Loch Morar at the west end of Glen Pean

Loch nan Uamh near Glen Beasdale

Their route was 'over inacessible mountains' and 'by the cruelest road yt cou'd be seen.' At four in the morning, they reached the head of Loch Morar, where they sent for a boat to complete the journey to the coast. When the boat had not arrived by the late afternoon, they set off walking again 'through ways as bad as before' and 'past one of the highest & wildest mountains'. Eventually, they stopped at Meoble, and were accommodated in the bothy of Angus MacEachine, who, as well as being a surgeon in Charles' army, was Borrodale's son-in-law. They were fed on 'some milk, cruds, & butter.' Charles 'eat of it as if he had the best cheer yt ever he made'. Although they now had the horses again, it was impossible to use them for the route ahead. They therefore walked the rest of the way to Loch nan Uamh, where they arrived about four o' clock in the afternoon of 20 April. Charles was received by Borrodale, who provided meal, lamb and butter to eat, as well as straw to sleep on. Borrodale's wife gave Charles a new suit of Highland clothes. He was accommodated in a cottage in Glen Beasdale.

Charles quickly contacted Aeneas MacDonald, one of the original 'Seven Men of Moidart'. Aeneas was now at Kinlochmoidart after having collected some gold left by a Spanish supply ship at Barra. On learning of Charles' intention to sail to the Outer Isles, Aeneas immediately wrote back recommending his own pilot, 68-year-old Donald MacLeod. Donald was duly summoned to Borrodale.

Donald met Charles purely by chance walking alone in a wood. Somehow, Charles guessed who Donald was.

'Are you Donald MacLeod of Guatergill in Sky?' he asked.

'Yes,' said Donald, 'I am the same man, may it please your Majesty, at your service. What is your pleasure wi' me?'

'Then,' said the Prince, 'You see, Donald,

I am in distress. I therefore throw myself in your bosom, and let you do with me what you like. I hear you are an honest man, and fit to be trusted.'

'Alas, may it please your excellency, what can I do for you? For I am but a poor auld man, and can do very little for mysell.'

'Why,' said the Prince, 'the service I am to put you upon I know you can perform very well. It is that you may go with letters from me to Sir Alexander MacDonald and the Laird of MacLeod. I desire therefore to know if you will undertake this piece of service: for I am really convinced that these gentlemen for all that they have done, will do all in their power to protect me.'

'What', said Donald, 'does not your excellency know that these men have played the rogue to you altogether, and will you trust them for a' that? Na, you mauna do 't.'

Donald explained that, just a few miles away, these two chiefs were at that very moment leading their forces in search of Charles. Donald refused to take any message from Charles to them, and urged Charles to leave Borrodale as soon as possible.

Charles then changed his request, saying that he wanted to go to the Isle of Lewis, where he hoped to charter a ship at Stornoway.

'I hear, Donald, you are a good pilot; that you know all this coast well, and therefore I hope you can carry me safely through the islands where I may look for more safety that I can do here.' Donald replied that he would do anything in the world for Charles.

The only available craft was an eight-oared boat that had been sunk in the loch during a raid by government troops some time ago. Work immediately began on its salvage and repair.

Over the next few days, survivors from Culloden gradually made their way into the area. Young Clanranald, Barrisdale and John Hay, who had replaced the sick Murray of Broughton, as Charles' secretary, arrived at Borrodale. Murray of Broughton,

Sheridan and Dr Archibald Cameron, who was Lochiel's brother, went to the head of Loch Arkaig. Lochiel, with both ankles broken by grapeshot, was carried to Achnacarry on horseback.

There was general dismay when they learned that Charles wanted to leave Scotland. Young Clanranald offered to build four bothies in which Charles could hide in different woods. Lochiel sent Dr Archibald Cameron with a letter imploring Charles not to leave. However, Charles was influenced more by O'Sullivan and Father MacDonald, who were urging him to leave. He would not even accept Young Clanranald's compromise offer to go to the Outer Isles himself in search of a ship.

Gradually, news arrived that some of the clans were giving themselves up. There were also rumours that some chiefs, including Barrisdale, had started to collude with the enemy. On learning that the government troops had advanced along the whole of the Great Glen, Charles realised that he was now completely cut off from the clans in Badenoch. It was now impossible for him to muster them. With only two hundred troops at Borrodale, there were not enough to renew the campaign.

After a few days, Charles learned that government troops, under Lord Loudoun, were about to sail from Skye to scour the area where Charles now was. On 26 April, Charles decided to leave immediately with O'Sullivan and Father MacDonald. In the absence of Alexander MacLeod, his aide-de-camp, Charles recruited Captain Felix O'Neil, who had originally been sent from France with a strong personal recommendation from Charles' brother.

Before leaving, Charles sent Sheridan a post-dated letter that he wanted to be shown to the clan chiefs.

FOR THE CHIEFS.

When I came to this Country, it was my only view to do all in my power for your good and safety. This I will allways do as long as life is in me. But alas! I see with grief, I can at present do little for you on this side the water, for the only thing that can be done, is to defend your selves till the French assist you. If not, to be able to make better terms. To effectuate this, the only way is to assemble in a body as soon as possible, and then take measures for the best, which you that know the Country are only Judges of. This makes me be of little use here, whereas by my going into France instantly, however dangerous it be, I will certainly engage the French Court either to assist us effectually and powerfully, or at least to procure you such terms as you would not obtain otherways. My presence there, I flatter myself, will have more effect to bring this sooner to a determination that any body else, for several reasons, one of which I will mention here, vizt. It is thought to be a Politick, tho' a false one, of the French Court, not to restore our Master, but to keep a continual civil war in this country, which renders the English government less powerfull and, of consequence, themselves more. This is absolutely destroyed by my leaving this Country, which nothing else but this will persuade them that this Play cannot last, and if not remedied, the Elector will soon be as despotick as the French King, which I should think will oblige them to strike the great stroke, which is always in their power, however, averse they may have been to it for the time past. Before leaving off, I must recommend to you that all things should be decided by a Councill of all your Chiefs, or, in any of your absence, the next Commander of your several corps, with the assistance of the Duke of Perth and Lord George Murray, who I am persuaded, will stick by you to the very last.

My departure should be kept as long private and concealed as possible on one pretext or other, which you will fall upon. May the Almighty bless and direct you.'

(28 April, 1746)

3
26 - 30 APRIL
BORRODALE to BENBECULA

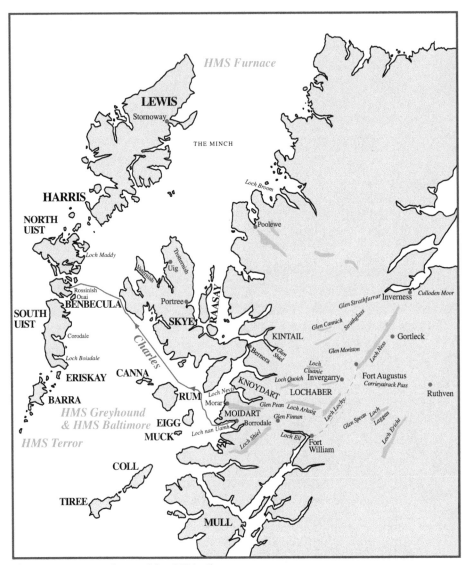

The various movements between 26 and 30 April

The events now follow three related threads. First, there are the attempts of the enemy trying to capture Charles. Secondly, there are the exploits of Charles' various friends trying to help him escape to France. Thirdly, there are the adventures of the Prince himself.

The Enemy

The immediate threats to Charles were the forces of General John Campbell. His command covered the army and naval units that had been positioned for some months in the Western Highlands to prevent ships supplying the rebels.

The flotilla of government ships patrolling the Minch was commanded by Captain Thomas Noel from the 24-gun frigate, *Greyhound*. There were also HMS *Furnace*, *Terror*, *Serpent*, *Baltimore*, and *Raven*, all sloops with a dozen or so cannons, and a similar number of swivel guns. At this time, the north and south entrances to the Minch were being guarded by Captain John Fergussone in the *Furnace*, and Captain Robert Duff in the *Terror*. Noel, himself, was cruising between them in the *Greyhound*, accompanied by Captain Richard Howe in the *Baltimore*.

General John Campbell of Mamore

A Frigate

33

On Skye, Lord Loudoun had been training a large force of raw militia he had led there after the ignominious rout at Moy in February. He was now about to comply with Cumberland's orders in leading his men across to the mainland, and up the Great Glen to Fort Augustus. On the way, he had to 'drive the cattel and burn the plowes of all those that either are or have been out in the rebellion and to distress them in every other way and to burn the houses of there leaders'.

The Friends

Rouillée and Lory in *Le Mars* and *La Bellone* were now approaching the west coast of Scotland. In planning this expedition, Walsh knew very well the strength of the Royal Navy ships patrolling the area. He had therefore chosen the two ships that could deal with any opposition they might meet. They were larger than the British ships, and, with 36 guns each, they had superior firepower. In addition, they carried a combined force of some seven hundred men.

The Prince

The Prince's companions:
Colonel John
O'Sullivan,
Captain Felix O'Neil,
Father Allan
MacDonald,
Edward Burke and
Donald MacLeod.

Donald MacLeod's crew included his 15-year-old son, Murdoch, Ned Burke, and six other men recruited by Clanranald and Borrodale.

They were Roderick MacDonald, Lauchlan MacMurrich, Roderick MacCasgill, John MacDonald, Duncan Roy, and Alexander MacDonald.

To reduce the chances of detection by the Royal Navy, Donald intended to make the sailing overnight. He planned to set off about eight o'clock, while there was still enough light to steer clear of the rocks in Loch nan Uamh.

A sloop

As the time approached, Donald was alarmed at the gathering storm clouds, and wanted to postpone the departure. However, Charles, determined, as he was, to leave that night, rejected Donald's advice.

They set sail, with Donald at the helm, and Charles sitting in the bottom of the boat between Donald's legs. They had not rowed far from the shore when the rain began to pour, and the wind reached gale force. O'Sullivan asked Donald what he thought of the weather now.

'I think nothing yts good of it, & wish we cou'd get back, but it is not possible; if the wind does not change, the boat is good & we have good hands.'

Within half an hour, a violent thunder storm broke, and large waves crashed over the sides of the boat. To everyone's relief, Charles now asked Donald to steer for the shore.

'I had rather face canons and muskets than be in such a storm as this.'

Much as Donald wanted to obey Charles, he refused to do so.

'Why, since we are here we have nothing for it, but under God, to set out to sea directly. Is it not as good for us to be drown'd in clean water as to be dashed in pieces upon a rock and to be drowned too?'

He tried to assure everyone that the storm would be over soon. However, the storm grew worse. Donald had to let the boat run before the wind. In the pitch-blackness, every man was silent, knowing that the slightest side-wind would overturn them, and that the next gigantic wave could swamp the boat completely. As it was, the boat was quickly filling up with water. Charles, clinging to a plank, stood shouting orders for everyone to bail. One wave threw Charles across the boat, flattening him against the side. As O'Sullivan and O'Neil went to help

him, another enormous wave sent all three of them sprawling, and filled the boat with water. Some members of the crew thought the boat was now lost, and began to pray aloud. Immediately Charles recovered, he ordered the men to continue bailing, and told them to let Father MacDonald do the praying. Despite a lifetime in these waters, Donald MacLeod had never experienced a storm as violent as this. He was trembling with fear, and could hardly hold the helm. Charles told the terrified O'Sullivan to stay by Donald's side, and encourage him.

Although the storm raged throughout the night, they survived. By daylight, they were off the coast of Benbecula, where they decided to try and find a safe place to land. As they approached the Rossinish peninsula, the wind strengthened, blowing the boat out of control towards a small island. Frantically, the men tried to pull the sail down, but the wet ropes jammed round the mast. With the boat careering towards destruction on the rocks, all hands prepared to jump into the water. At the last second, 'as if God set his hand to it, one man touched the seal & it fell down in a minuit, when three or four cou'd not get it down a moment before'. Roderick MacDonald was then able to steer the boat through calmer waters to land on the shore of Loch Uiskevagh.

Their arrival was noticed by a herdsman who lived in an isolated shiely hut close by. Seeing these strangers to be fully armed, he immediately ran away, deserting his cattle.

Charles and his friends staggered through the gale to the hut, where, wet from head to toe, and black with cold, they collapsed from exhaustion. As they recovered, they could do nothing but talk of the danger they had just endured. The experience they had shared had removed all class barriers between them.

'In that moment all were compagions.'

Eventually, they roused themselves to make a fire, and start preparing a meal. An iron cooking pot, that Donald had brought in the boat, was found to have a hole as large as half a crown in the bottom.

' "Il shew it up," says one of the men, takes some rags he had, roulles them up as they were, clean or durty, makes two or three smal hols, about the large one wth his dork, stops this hole wth his rags & shews them up with other rags.'

They then placed the pot directly on the fire to make brochan, a porridge-like gruel. which 'the Prince took of it, as if there were no rags in the pot'. Their only other food was some butter, cheese and half a lamb. As this was insufficient for the whole party, Charles ordered one of his men to shoot a cow belonging to the herdsman, who had fled on their arrival. Charles also announced that he would pay for it. After the meal, Charles slept on a bed made from an old sail spread on the bare ground.

Meanwhile, the herdsman had run the seven miles to Nunton, where his master, Old Clanranald, was having dinner with several guests, including the schoolmaster, Neil MacEachain, and a minister, Rev. John MacAuley from South Uist. On hearing the herdsman's report, Old Clanranald wanted to investigate. Although he was only 53-years-old, Old Clanranald was so senile and racked with rheumatism, that he was unable to make the journey himself. He sent his second son, Donald during a lull in the storm. At the same time, MacAuley, who was a Hanoverian supporter, secretly sent his own man on the same errand.

On the way, Donald met Allan MacDonald, who had been sent by Charles to meet Old Clanranald. Thus, Donald learned for certain that Charles had landed on Benbecula. Allan also informed Donald that Charles wanted Old Clanranald to come and see him before they left for Stornoway that night. By pretending that he also had been sent by Old Clanranald, MacAuley's spy learned of Charles' plans from Allan MacDonald as well.

The storm resumed, and continued for three days. During this time, Charles had to stay where he was. On the second day, Old Clanranald sent his son with biscuits, meal and butter. On the third day, when the storm slackened, Old Clanranald, accompanied by Neil MacEachain, made a secret courtesy visit. That night, Charles and his party set sail for Stornoway.

Although there were no government troops in Stornoway, it was obvious that the offer of a £30,000 reward may well tempt some of the local residents into handing Charles over to the authorities. Charles and his friends therefore concocted a story to hide his identity, and to explain their sudden arrival in such a distressed condition. Thus, Charles, O' Sullivan, Allan MacDonald and O'Neil were to pass themselves off as survivors from a merchant ship wrecked in the storm. O'Sullivan was to be the merchant, 'Sinclair', and Charles his son, 'William'. Allan MacDonald, under the name 'Dalrymple' was to be the mate of the ship, and O'Neil, wearing Highland dress, was renamed 'MacNeil'. In their story, they had met Donald MacLeod in Barra, en route to Caithness to buy meal. He had undertaken to take them in his boat to Stornoway, where they could get a ship to the Orkneys.

The end of the Rossinish peninsula

4

30 APRIL - 6 MAY
BENBECULA to LEWIS

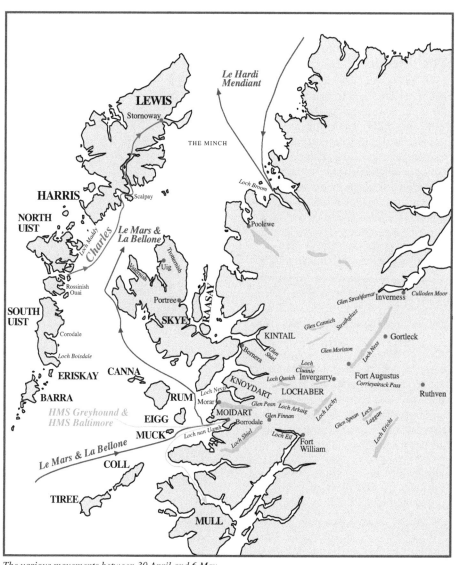

The various movements between 30 April and 6 May

The Enemy

Rev. John MacAuley MacAuley had sent a letter to his father on Harris, asking that Rev. Colin MacKenzie, a Hanoverian supporter living near Stornoway, should be informed of Charles' intentions. He also urged that arrangements should be made for Charles to be apprehended on arriving at Stornoway.

The Friends

Rouillée and Lory *Le Mars* and *La Bellone* entered the Minch at the tail end of the storm. Undetected by the Royal Navy, they reached Loch nan Uamh on 30 April, and unloaded gold, weapons and ammunition. On 1 May, Captain Noel at Ornsay was informed about the arrival of the French ships. The news also travelled quickly to the head of Loch Arkaig, where Murray of Broughton and Dr Archibald Cameron immediately set off to meet the officers from the French ships. When Murray learned their purpose, Alexander MacLeod was deputed to accompany the ships to find Charles in the Outer Isles.

On 3 May, HMS *Greyhound*, *Terror* and *Baltimore* hurried to Loch nan Uamh, where they engaged the two French ships. After a battle of six hours, the British ships departed to the Sound of Mull, very much the worse for the encounter. The French ships were also badly damaged. In order to avoid a second battle, they weighed anchor next day, taking several Jacobite leaders, including Lord Elcho, Sir Thomas Sheridan, and his nephew, Captain Michael Sheridan. As the English ships had gone south, the French headed north. The plan to look for Charles in the islands was abandoned. Instead, they were to round the Butt of Lewis, and escape into the Atlantic.

Some of the gold, that the French ships had delivered, was promptly stolen by Barrisdale in the first of his various treacherous deeds. The remainder was conveyed, under the supervision of Murray of Broughton, to the head of Loch Arkaig

Dumont Further up the coast, the cutter, *Le Hardi Mendiant,* arrived on 1 May at Loch Broom. When the residents broke the news of Culloden, the ship's captain, Mathieu Dumont, left Captain Lynch and Lieutenant ('Spanish John') MacDonnell with orders to find Charles, and deliver dispatches from Charles' brother, as well as £3,000 in gold. Meanwhile, Dumont sailed immediately for France, intending to return in a few weeks to collect his two men and, perhaps, Charles.

The Prince

As it was too dangerous to be at sea during the day, Charles and his party landed on the island of Scalpay early in the morning. The only resident, Donald Campbell, who was a friend of Donald MacLeod, provided accommodation.

'The Prince was very well in this honest mans house, there was a kind of a bed & clean sheets, but the Prince made but very little use of sheets & lay alwaise in his Cloaths; he had good barley bread, yt he eat of hartilly, good milk, butter & eggs, & lamb, we all forgot our past misery here, thought our selfs happy.'

The next day, Donald MacLeod borrowed a small sailing boat from Donald Campbell, and set off with his boatmen to hire a ship at Stornoway. Over the next two days, Charles, using the name, 'William Sinclair', amused himself fishing with Donald Campbell's young son, Kenneth, who persistently embarrassed Charles with searching, but ingenuous, questions about the details of the recent ship wreck. Charles also explored the island. One evening, he single-handedly rescued a cow stuck in a bog.

On 4 May, a letter arrived from Donald MacLeod, announcing that he had procured a brig, and requesting Charles to come to Stornoway immediately.

The north harbour, Scalpay

Leaving Allan MacDonald to return to South Uist, Charles, O'Neil, O'Sullivan and Ned Burke set off at night in a boat with Donald's son, a boatman and a guide. Whereas Donald MacLeod had sailed all the way to Stornoway, Charles intended to sail only up Loch Seaforth, and walk the remaining eighteen miles. From the head of the loch, he aimed to be aboard the brig before daybreak. Unfortunately, the weather was very bad, and they got lost.

> 'The Guide did not know in the world where he was, in the wildest contry in the universe, nothing but moors & lochs, not a house in sight, nor the least marque of a road or path, walking all night with a continual heavy rain.'

After going eight miles out of their way, they reached the outskirts of Stornoway at about eleven o'clock in the morning. Having spent some seven hours walking, they were all exhausted, as well as cold, and soaked to the skin. The terrain was so rough that Charles' shoes had fallen to pieces, and had to be tied together with laces.

> 'His toes were were quit stript.'

Loch Seaforth from the north

The guide was sent to inform Donald MacLeod of Charles' arrival. Meanwhile, Charles and his friends could only wait, 'exposed to the same rain without the least shelter, not dareing to lift up their heads'. While Donald went to Stornoway to finalise the arrangements for the hire of the brig, he sent his son to Charles with brandy, bread and cheese. Later, one of Donald's crew arrived to guide Charles and his friends to Kildun House at Arnish, just two miles south of Stornoway. Here, they warmed themselves by a good fire, and began to dry their sodden clothes. The owner of the house, Colin MacKenzie, was away, but his wife provided milk, eggs, butter, biscuits, whisky, clean straw and blankets.

> 'Who cou'd be happyer, but this satisfaction did not lasst long.'

After Donald MacLeod struck the bargain with the captain of the brig, both men went on to a celebratory bout of drinking. In the process, Donald revealed the true identity of 'William Sinclair'. Knowing what the punishments would be for helping Charles to escape, the captain changed his mind overnight, and now refused to let Donald hire the ship at all.

To make matters worse, Donald also learned that, on receiving MacAuley's letter, Rev. MacKenzie had spread the rumour that Charles with five hundred men was about to plunder the town, and seize a ship. As a result, three hundred townsmen had now taken to arms.

Donald went to meet their officers in order to put the facts straight.

'Where, I pray you,' said he, 'could the Prince in his present condition get 500 or one hundred men together? I believe the men are mad. Has the devil possessed you altogether?'

After some very heated exchanges, Donald was unable to convince them otherwise.

'Well then, since you know already that the Prince is upon your island, I acknowledge the truth of it; but then he is so far from having any number of men with him that he has only but two companions with him, and when I am there I make the third. And yet let me tell you farther, gentlemen, if Seaforth himself were here, by G— —- he durst not put a hand to the Prince's breast.'

The officers assured Donald that they had no intention of harming Charles. They simply wanted Charles to leave the island. However, they refused to provide a pilot at any price.

In the evening, Donald reported the grim news to Charles and his friends. Their first reaction was to leave immediately. However, none of them was in a fit state to walk, and the weather was too bad to go by boat. Mrs MacKenzie arranged for close friends to keep watch, so that 'if a soul stured out of the town, yt she would be informed of it in a moment'. Fortunately, Charles and his friends were not disturbed in the night, and they were able to sleep.

By dawn, they could hear drums beating in the town. Their scouts informed them that the townsfolk now knew where Charles was. Later, over a hundred men converged on Kildun house. Ned Burke advised the Prince to take to the mountains. Charles, however, was very composed.

Loch Arnish

'How long is it, Ned, since you turned cowardly? I shall be sure of the best of them ere taken, which I hope shall be never in life.'

Charles went out and faced the crowd, which then dispersed.

Despite this victory, it was obviously too dangerous to stay. Sooner or later, someone would inform the army. Charles' party therefore made preparations to leave next morning, using the boat that Donald MacLeod had sailed from Scalpay.

They bought several pairs of new shoes to replace those ruined on the walk from Loch Seaforth. Mrs MacKenzie gave Charles a blanket, and also had a cow killed. At first, she refused to accept any payment, but Donald MacLeod insisted that she should.

> 'For so long as there was any money among us, I was positive that the deel a man or woman should have it to say that the Prince ate their meat for nought.'

They took the head, and other pieces, together with some, meal, brandy and sugar. They also took a wooden plate for making dough, and some stones 'for birsling their bannocks before the fire'.

5
6 - 14 MAY
LEWIS to BENBECULA

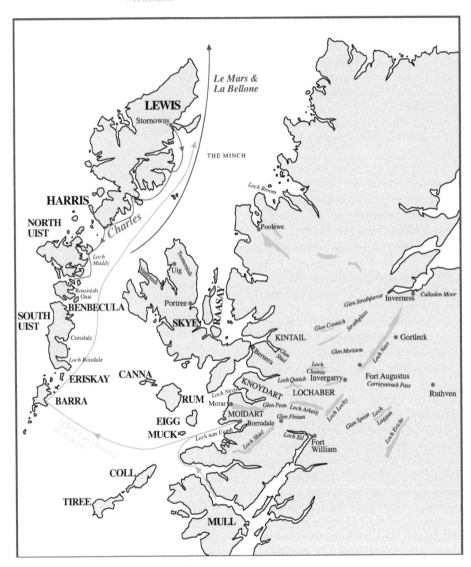

The various movements between 6 and 14 May

The Enemy

For the Royal Navy, the arrival of *La Bellone* and *Le Mars* meant two imminent dangers. First, Charles and other prominent rebels may escape in these ships. Secondly, it was known that the ships had delivered supplies and possibly soldiers that could renew hostilities. Captain Noel therefore set out to capture or destroy the two French ships. Captain John Fergussone in the *Furnace* was given the task of finding what they had left behind.

Noel At his anchorage in the Sound of Mull, Captain Noel was confident that the two French ships had been so badly damaged that they would not be able to leave Loch nan Uamh for some days. He immediately prepared for another battle with them. By 6 May, Noel's ships were repaired, and, reinforced by the *Raven,* they all set off for Loch nan Uamh. On learning that the French ships had left two days previously, Noel wrongly assumed that they had sailed south, and led his flotilla in pursuit. When he reached Barra without sighting the enemy, he turned north. On 9 May, off Stornoway, he gave up the chase.

He then began to cruise down the east side of the Outer Hebrides with the *Raven* and *Terror* in attendance. On the way, they came across several small sailing boats, which they approached to inspect who and what was on board. Many of these boats avoided the encounters by escaping into shallows or inlets. On 14 May, Noel heard of the arrival of *Le Hardi Mendiant* at Loch Broom. Leaving the *Raven* to guard the southern approaches to the Minch, the *Greyhound* and the *Terror* set off to investigate. On the way, they met HMS *Scarborough, Glasgow, Happy Jennet,* and *Tryall,* coming to reinforce the blockade of the west coast.

Fergussone After a brief visit to Loch nan Uamh, Fergussone's brutal investigations led him to believe that the French ships had landed three hundred men together with money, arms and ammunition. Fergussone also concluded that the arms and supplies would now be in the possession of Barrisdale. He therefore sailed round to Loch Nevis, where he bombarded the township on the north shore. In the process, Barrisdale's house was destroyed. Some days later, Fergussone raided the settlements by Loch Ailort, where a prisoner revealed that Charles had recently sailed in a small boat to the islands.

Fergussone next attacked the island of Raasay.

'He ordered on Lieutenant Dalrumple ashore to execute his vengeance againstthe island who brunt Rasay's good house to ashes,
as also the whole houses upon the island, excepting two small villages that escaped their sight, with all the poor people's furniture. The number of the houses brunt, according to a strict accompt taken of them, exceeded three hundred. They likewise found all Rasay's furniture and silver-plate hid in a cave about a quarter of a mile from the house, betrayed by a small boy belonging to the island........
They gathered what cattle was in their way, cows and horses, sheep and goats, and slaughtered numbers of all kinds, and left many of the dead both in the shores and hill.'

The Friends

The Scots On 8 May, there was a gathering of prominent rebels at the head of Loch Arkaig. They included Lord Lovat, Murray of Broughton, Lochiel, Archibald Cameron, Young Clanranald, Lochgarry, Barrisdale, Old MacKinnon, John Roy Stewart, Alexander MacLeod, and Sir Stewart Threpland.

Despite Charles' departure, they resolved to use the French gold to continue the struggle against the Hanoverian troops. The western clans were to gather at Achnacarry. A letter was sent to Cluny asking him to muster the eastern clans in Badenoch.

Lynch and Spanish John For a few days, Lynch and Spanish John stayed on the shores of Loch Broom with some MacKenzies. There, they learned that the most likely place to find Charles was somewhere near Lochiel's estate in Lochaber. They set off, with Spanish John, a native of Knoydart, leading the way. Soon, they discovered that half the gold they were carrying was missing. Convinced that it had been stolen at Loch Broom, they retraced their steps in order to retrieve it. However, the MacKenzies professed total ignorance of the theft. After much acrimony, Lynch and Spanish John resumed their journey south, without recovering the stolen gold.

The Prince

The Prince's companions:
Colonel John O'Sullivan,
Captain Felix O'Neil, Edward
Burke, and Donald MacLeod.

Still hoping to find a ship that would take him to France, Charles now planned to sail to Loch Broom on the mainland. Apart from Donald MacLeod, the boatmen were not aware of this plan, until they were well out to sea. When they were informed of the proposed destination, they refused to go any further, fearing that their boat would founder in the slightest gale. During the

The island of Iubhard

ensuing argument, they were all alarmed to see two men-of-war heading towards them from the south. They headed as fast as they could for the nearest shore, which was Iubhard, a small island off the east coast of Harris.

From the top of a hill, Charles and his friends watched the ships sail past. The two ships were *Le Mars* and *La Bellone* escaping from Loch nan Uamh. From the characteristic rigging, Charles recognised that they were in fact French. He therefore urged the crew to sail out to

the ships, and find out. However, some of the crew were equally convinced that the ships were English. Once again, they refused to obey his orders. Had they done so, Charles would have been rescued immediately.

As soon as the ships were out of sight, Charles and his friends re-embarked. Hardly had they set off, when they spied another two ships, so they returned to the safety of Iubhard. When yet two more ships appeared on the horizon, they decided to spend the night on the island.

They found a small hut, that had been hastily abandoned by some fishermen, who feared that Charles and his party might be a press-gang. As the hut was built like a pig-sty, with no proper entrance, Charles' boatmen had to break down part of the structure in order to enter. They gathered heather to make beds as well as a fire, and spread the sail over the roof to keep out the rain. That night, the weather turned bad. The continuous gales confined them to Iubhard for four days and nights.

In some ways, the party kept up the formal relationships between the social classes. For example, only Charles and the gentlemen slept in the hut. They also ate separately. In other ways, the barriers were broken down completely, with Ned Burke engaging in banter and practical jokes at Charles' expense. Charles was also enthusiastic about joining with all the improvisations they had to make.

'Never any meat or drink came wrong to him, for he could take a share of every thing, be it good, bad, or indifferent, and was always chearful and contented in every condition.'

There were no cooking or eating utensils in this primitive hovel, so Charles kept shells in his pockets for use both as cups and spoons. As there was only one wooden bowl, everyone had to wait for turn to drink brochan from it.

'Yt was the only thing yt repugned him, for he is not dellicate in any thing else.'

Charles often helped Ned Burke do the cooking. In fact, Charles' inventive recipes and improvised methods made him best cook in the party. He mixed cow's brains and meal to bake 'very good bread indeed'. He salvaged some butter that Ned wanted to throw away. During the journey from Arnish, it had been 'betwixt two fardles of bread', which had crumbled thereby making the butter of 'a very ugly appearance'.

'What,' said the Prince, 'Was not the butter clean when it was put there?'

'Yes,' said Ned, 'It was clean enough.'

'Then,' replied the Prince, 'You are a child, Ned. The butter will do exceedingly well. The bread can never file it. Go fetch it immediately.'

Looking out over the Minch from Iubhard

Charles used the butter to cook cod and ling that had been left to dry in heaps strewn over the shore. Unfortunately, Donald MacLeod was revolted by the sight of 'fish and the crumbs of bread swimming among the butter.'

> 'The deel a drap of that butter he would take, for it was neither good nor clean.'

However, Charles insisted that they should all try it. In the end, all agreed it made 'a very hearty meal'.

For drink, they made a punch by heating brandy and sugar in an earthen pitcher that they found in the hut. However, when the pitcher was accidentally broken, they had to resort to spring water. Whatever they were drinking, Charles often gave them the toast 'Black Eye', his pet name for the daughter of the King of France.

By the fifth day, the weather was suitable to leave. They decided to set sail in the evening. Their intended destination was Benbecula, where Charles hoped that Old Clanranald would give them protection. Charles wanted to take some fish from the piles on the shore, and leave money in payment for the men who owned it. However, O'Sullivan and O'Neil advised him that the money would probably be taken by vagrants before the fishermen returned. He therefore decided to abandon the whole idea.

The first port of call was Scalpay, where they arrived about one o'clock in the morning. Here, Charles hoped to persuade Donald Campbell to hire them the boat in which they were sailing, because it was 'such a fine, light, swift-sailing thing'. Unfortunately, Donald had recently fled from Scalpay. It was common knowledge that he had recently harboured the Prince, and he feared reprisals from the authorities. While they were deliberating on the shore, Ned Burke noticed four men approaching. Whistling to alert his friends, he went towards the strangers. On closer inspection, he became very suspicious. He rushed back to the boat, and, vaulting aboard, he urged Charles to leave immediately. Charles' boatmen then rowed away as fast as they could, and continued their journey south along the coast of Harris.

At daybreak, the wind rose, so they were able to hoist the sail. Later that morning, they were alarmed by HMS *Furnace* suddenly appearing out of Loch Finsbay. She was actually 'within two musket shots' before they noticed her. They set off under full sail with the *Furnace* in pursuit. After about four miles, they rowed into a bay near Rodil point. As the tide was ebbing, the water in the bay was too shallow for the sloop. The sloop sailed away.

In the evening, there was a similar scare off the coast of North Uist, where HMS *Terror* was about to sail out of Loch Maddy. Immediately, she fired two guns as a signal for Charles' boat to heave to. This time, the fugitives thought there was no escape, because they were well in range of the sloop's cannons. Nevertheless, they rowed frantically away. Eventually, they lost their pursuers among the little islands between North Uist and Benbecula.

During the night, they were all faint from hunger and thirst. They soaked meal in salt water to make drammach, which Charles thought was 'no bad food', and drank brandy. The next day, they sailed down Benbecula, and landed once again in Loch Uiskevagh.

Soon afterwards, the weather changed to bring gale-force winds and heavy rain. Miserable though it was, they were consoled by the direction of the

wind, that prevented the sloops from entering Loch Uiskevagh. Under the shelter of a rock, they lit a fire to make brochan, and cook crabs that they caught in the rocks by the shore.

When they realised that the storm was set to continue for some time, one of the boatmen led them to Rairnish, where they found 'a poor grasskeeper's bothy or hut which had so laigh a door that we digged below the door and put heather below the Prince's knees, he being so tall, to let him go the easier into the poor hut'. A messenger was then sent to inform Old Clanranald of their arrival. Meanwhile, they occupied themselves catching fish, and shooting fowl. Being a regular smoker, Charles was continually breaking the stems of his pipes. He improvised a method of repair with quills to make 'cutties' which allowed 'the tobacco to smoak cool'.

Next day, Old Clanranald arrived with Neil MacEachain. They brought wine, beer, biscuits, and trout.

'Never a man was welcomer,
to be sure.'

Old Clanranald assured Charles that there was nothing to fear. He also agreed to find a suitable hiding place, and give the necessary protection. He made a list of food and clothes that Charles needed. However, Charles declined Old Clanranald's offer of bedsheets.

Charles 'showd him his plad & blanquet, & said he'd have no other, yt he was a highlander, but yt if he cou'd get him highland Cloaths yt he'd be obliged to him'. Old Clanranald then left to make the arrangements.

The supplies duly arrived the following day. In addition to four shirts, some stockings, and a pair of shoes, there was a silver cup with a cover. Using this, Charles no longer had to drink from the communal bowl. The news of Charles' arrival also reached Allan MacDonald, who rejoined Charles.

For the next two days, Charles appeared very buoyant, and gave the impression that 'every thing was good, everything relished with him'. However, O'Sullivan recognised that this behaviour was just a cover for a bad state of depression. Charles' mood was not helped by a rumour about the two French ships that had come and gone without trying to find him on the islands. When O'Sullivan tried to humour Charles by reserving the wine and beer for him alone, Charles refused it, saying that he 'woud not teast of, if those yt were wth him did not drink as fair as he did of it, & were oblidged to do it'.

On 14 May, Neil MacEachain arrived to take Charles to South Uist, where he had two cottages in Corodale, a remote valley on the east coast of the island. Before setting off, Charles ordered Donald MacLeod and Allan MacDonald to go to the mainland. Their mission was to seek information about what was happening there, and deliver letters to Murray of Broughton and Lochiel. They were also commissioned to bring back money and brandy.

6
14 MAY - 5 JUNE
BENBECULA to SOUTH UIST

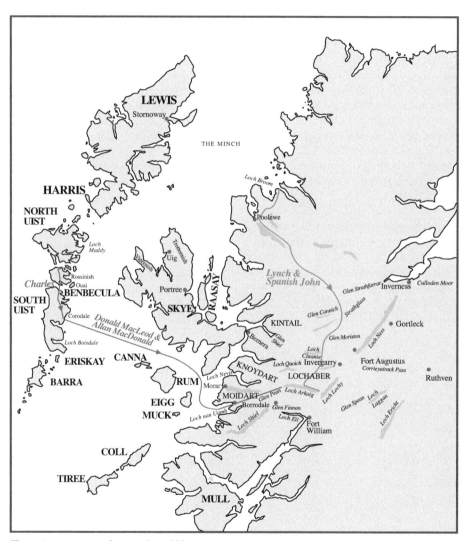

The various movements between 14 and 22 May

The Enemy

On 14 May, the ships patrolling the Minch were reinforced by HMS *Scarborough*, *Glasgow*, *Happy Jennet*, and *Tryall*. Noel was now confident he could prevent supply ships reaching the rebels, and intercept all fleeing fugitives. At the same time as searching for Charles, the Hanoverian forces set about breaking the spirit of the clans that had taken part in the rebellion. The Royal Navy aimed their retribution at the Clanranald MacDonalds on the mainland. On 17 May, Fergussone raided the area round the Morar estuary, and burned the house of Macdonald of Morar. Next, Fergussone and Duff attacked the settlements on the shores of Loch nan Uamh, razing every house. Then, they dealt similar treatment to the villages by Loch Ailort, where they also slaughtered all the cattle. Later, they resumed their patrol of the Minch. On 21 May, the *Terror* put into Stornoway, where the residents informed Duff that Charles had actually been there just over a fortnight previously.

The Friends

The Scots While the chiefs at the head of Loch Arkaig waited for the clans to gather at Achnacarry, it was resolved to bury the gold from the two French ships in two secret locations on the south side of Loch Arkaig. As recorded in the accounts of Murray of Broughton, one of the sites was in Gleann Camgharaidh.

> 'This sum of 15,000 louis-dores in each bag, counted over exactly, was divided into three parcels, 500 in each, one parcel put under a rock in a small rivulet, the other two parcels in the ground at a little distance, the holes made and the money deposited by Sir Stewart Thriepland, Mr Alexander M'Leod yor of Neuck, Major Kennedy and Dr Cameron.'

The other site was near the east end of Loch Arkaig, where, on 22 May, Archibald Cameron and Alexander MacLeod carried 'two parcels 6000 in each, all in bags of 1000 each' on their shoulders from Achnacarry.

Corodale

Lynch and Spanish John After their bitter experience of being robbed, the two officers from *Le Hardi Mendiant* made their way warily to the house of Lady Dundonnell, just a few miles from Loch Broom. As well as giving them food and shelter, she ordered half a dozen armed men to guard their baggage. The next day, she provided guides for the rest of their journey.

After several days, they reached the head of Loch Arkaig on 22 May. There, they encountered Barrisdale, and learned that the Prince had left the mainland. They continued to Achnacarry, where they met Lochiel, and delivered the letters, together with the remaining 500 guineas of the gold to Murray of Broughton. Murray recorded the transaction in his account book with all the vagueness and inaccuracy of a very sick man.

> 'From a French officer who had landed upon the East Coast with 2000 guineas.........................£1,000
>
> N.B. - This French officer was charged with 2000 guineas, but said he had 1000 taken from him as he passed thro' the Mackenzies' country, and gave in an account of deductions from the other thousand; but as Mr M. cannot charge his memory with the extent of the sum, he has charged himself with one thousand pounds, tho' he still thinks he did not receive quite so much'.

The Prince

The Prince's companions: Colonel John O'Sullivan, Captain Felix O'Neil, Edward Burke, and Neil MacEachain.

Accompanied by several of Clanranald's men, Charles and his companions set off walking at eleven o'clock at night, and arrived at Corodale round about six the following evening. When they were within sight of the cottages, MacEachain decided to make sure that there was no danger of an ambush. He left Charles under a rock, while he went on alone. Fortunately, the only person at the cottage was MacEachain's own brother, Ranald, who had come the day before to prepare for Charles' arrival.

Compared to 'the abominable hole they had lately left', Charles' new residence 'look't like a palace'. Ranald had even made Charles a special seat of green turf, as well as a bed from heather and rushes. After a meal of bread, cheese and goat's milk, Charles had his feet washed, because they were 'extreme dirty, and very much galled by his night walk'. He then smoked a pipe before going to bed.

Now that he was in relative comfort and safety, Charles again turned his thoughts to finding a ship in which to escape.

All eyes, including those of the enemy, were on an Irish meal ship, *David*, which arrived in Loch Skiport. For the moment, Charles planned only to obtain supplies from the ship. He also arranged for meal to be stashed away in different parts of the island so that, no matter where he might be in the future, food would always be near at hand.

Apart from Old Clanranald, the only other person of influence in the area was Old Clanranald's stepbrother, Alexander MacDonald of Boisdale. Although, Boisdale had refused to 'come out' for Charles, he was known to be a Jacobite supporter at heart. Charles also knew that Boisdale had far more influence among the local populace than did Old Clanranald.

The next day, Charles sent O'Sullivan and Old Clanranald's son to contact Boisdale at Kilbride on the south coast of South Uist. The following evening, they returned, having obtained Boisdale's assurances of help. He had offered to try and hire a ship from Stornoway himself under the pretext of transporting kelp. In order to make detailed plans, it was necessary to meet Charles personally, but, as Boisdale knew that his movements would be watched by government informers, he asked for Charles to meet him near his home. O'Sullivan also reported that they had again heard the rumour about the two French ships leaving the mainland with Sir Thomas Sheridan on board.

As Charles could not believe that the ships would depart without coming to find him, he immediately arranged for James MacDonald, one of Clanranald's men, to sail to Loch nan Uamh, deliver a letter to Murray of Broughton, and find out the truth of the matter. Just before leaving, James asked Charles what he should do with the letter if he were apprehended by the enemy before delivering it. Charles demonstrated what

James should do with the letter in no uncertain terms!

'The Prince made it up by way of suppositer, and desir'd him drive it into his fundament.'

Meanwhile, Charles, went with O'Sullivan and Old Clanranald's son to meet Boisdale. They stayed near the entrance to Loch Boisdale for three or four days. During this time, Charles and Boisdale became firm friends in long drinking bouts out in the open. Boisdale agreed to correspond with Charles every day.

On returning to Corodale, Charles sent O'Neil and Old Clanranald's son to Stornoway. Their mission was to find a ship that would take them to France. They could inform Charles' brother where Charles was. In this way, the French would then know where to send a rescue ship.

22 May - 5 June
The Enemy

The Hanoverian campaign of vengeance continued on the coast and Inner Isles. It also gained momentum inland, as Cumberland moved his headquarters from Inverness to Fort Augustus. His first target was Achnacarry, where he knew the new force of clansmen was gathering.

Lord Loudoun's troops attacked in the morning of 23 May. The Cameron settlements at the east end of Loch Arkaig were devastated. Lochiel's house went up in flames. Next, it was the turn of the Grants in Glen Moriston, where Loudoun led the Skye militia in the company of the erstwhile Jacobites, Sir Alexander MacDonald of Sleat, and the Laird of MacLeod.

At the coast, a force led by Captain Fergussone devastated the island of Eigg. Having learned that Charles had been at Stornoway, General Campbell, the overall commander of the navy and army on the coast, now decided to search the Outer Isles. At the same time, the sloops would patrol the whole coastline to prevent Charles escaping by boat.

The islands of Lewis and Harris were being searched by troops commanded by Captain Fergussone and Captain MacKenzie. Further south, two hundred Skye militia, headed by Hugh MacDonald of Armadale and Alexander MacLeod of Ullinish, landed on Barra. Their next step was to cross to South Uist, where they were to guard the coastline, and await reinforcements.

The various movements between 22 May and 5 June

Armadale had lived for many years on South Uist after marrying the widow of MacDonald of Milton. He was a very close friend of Old Clanranald. Despite his current command as a captain in the Skye militia, Armadale was actually a Jacobite sympathiser. Indeed, he had been the first man to greet Charles after *La du Teillay* anchored in Loch nan Uamh the previous August. However, he had followed the example of his chief, Sir Alexander MacDonald, in not joining the rebellion. Ostensibly, he had remained loyal to the Hanoverian government.

The Friends

Fortunately, the men at Achnacarry were forewarned of Loudoun's onslaught, and most of them retreated safely to the head of Loch Arkaig. There, the chiefs realised it was useless to prolong the rebellion. The clansmen therefore disbanded.

Lynch and Spanish John On leaving Murray of Broughton, Lynch and Spanish John went to sleep with some of John's relatives at Achnacarry. When Loudoun attacked the following morning, Lynch and Spanish John joined the mass exodus to the head of Loch Arkaig.

The next day, they set off north, and made their way over several days to John's home in Knoydart. Lynch then went on alone towards Loch Broom, hoping to rendezvous with a French ship.

Donald MacLeod and Allan MacDonald After many hazards, Donald and Allan reached the head of Loch Arkaig, just after the clans dispersed. As Murray of Broughton and Lochiel were still there, the two messengers were able to deliver Charles' letters to them personally.

Although they were overjoyed to hear that Charles was still at large, Lochiel and Murray knew that he would eventually be caught in the islands. Murray undertook to sail to Corodale with Donald and Allan in order to persuade Charles to return to the mainland.

For reasons of security, Murray, accompanied by a Major Kennedy, made his way independently to the coast, where Donald and Allan joined him at their boat. Unfortunately, the journey took its toll on the very sick Murray. Realising that he was quite unfit for the boat journey, Murray decided not to continue to Corodale. The most he could do was to write Charles a letter recounting all the important developments on the mainland. It also implored Charles to come back to the mainland immediately, and advised him to sail to Eigg as a first step. As Donald set off to deliver the letter, he agreed to return immediately with a reply, if not with Charles himself. However, he advised Murray that Charles may have already escaped on the Irish meal ship.

Before leaving, Donald repeated Charles' request for money, but Murray refused, suspecting that Donald wanted the money for himself. He gave the excuse that 'he had none to give, having only about sixty louis d'ors to himself, which was not

worth the while to send'. However, Donald did succeed in carrying out Charles' other commission, and 'found means without much ado to purchase two anchors of brandy at a guinea per anchor'.

Lochiel Three weeks earlier, Lochiel had declined the opportunity to leave for France with *Le Mars* and *La Bellone*. As a matter of honour, he preferred to stay with his clansfolk. Now that the holocaust had begun, there was nothing he could do to support them. Like them, he could only look to his own safety, and try to escape from more ravages by Cumberland's army.

Lochiel left the head of Loch Arkaig soon after Murray departed for the coast. Travelling on horseback and by boat, he and some of his clansmen made their way in stages down the length of Loch Shiel to an island. A few days later, he was rejoined by Murray of Broughton.

Alexander MacLeod Being close to Lochiel and Murray of Broughton, Alexander MacLeod knew about the impending arrival of a rescue ship coming for Charles at Loch Broom. He hoped that he too could escape to France on it. He also knew that Cumberland's troops had not yet gone there in force. Compared to Lochaber, Loch Broom was a relatively safe place to be. He therefore began the long march north.

O'Neil O'Neil and Old Clanranald's son were escorted to Harris by Lady Clanranald. Almost as soon as they arrived there, O'Neil was recognised by someone who had seen him there with Charles a month before. Immediately, the alarm was raised, and O'Neil had to escape back to Benbecula with Lady Clanranald.

The French Although the news of Culloden had reached France early in May, the French court had decided not to make

an immediate attempt to rescue Charles, in case he had
been picked up by a supply ship. However, as soon as *Le
Mars*, *La Bellone* and *Le Hardi Mendiant* returned to
France, Louis went to great lengths to rescue Charles.
Three different rescue expeditions were now planned to set
off from Dunkirk. They were led respectively by Francois
Dumay, in the small sloop, *Le Lévrier
Volant*, Pierre Anguier, in the brigantine
Le Bien Trouvé, and Mathieu Dumont,
making his return journey in *Le Hardi
Mendiant*. By the end of May, Dumay
and Anguier had set off. Dumont was to
leave later in June.

The reports from the ships, that had
returned, suggested that Charles might be
found in one of two places. If Lynch had
been able to contact Charles, then it was
likely that Charles would be with Lynch,
on the west coast of the mainland.
However, if Lynch had failed to contact
Charles, Charles would probably still be in
the Outer Isles. All three expeditions were

Corodale from the east

bound for Loch Broom first. If necessary, they would
continue round the north of Lewis to the west coast of the
Outer Isles. By the beginning of June, *Le Lévrier Volant*
and *Le Bien Trouvé* had departed. They were followed by
Le Hardi Mendiant about two weeks later.

The beach at Corodale

and his friends had long discussions. Charles confided in MacEachain his conviction that the defeat at Culloden had been caused by betrayal of Lord George Murray, his commander-in-chief. On one walk, Charles fired a shot at a school of whales approaching the rock on which they were sitting. Convinced that he had killed one whale, he asked the reluctant MacEachain to swim out, and pull it ashore. However, as MacEachain began to undress, the whale swam off.

Corodale was a sportsman's paradise. Charles caught fish with hand lines, and shot game with his fusee. He impressed everyone with his prowess in shooting, 'papping down perhaps dozens in a day of muircocks and hens'. One day, he shot a deer 'offhand', as it ran straight towards him. However, his most spectacular feat was recounted by one of Clanranald's men, Lachlan MacDonald of Dremsdill,

> 'But one day as they happend to go
> a-hunting the Prince with his
> feusee in his hand stood on a
> hillside and whistled so exact that
> you coud not distinguish it from a

The Prince

The Prince's companions:
Colonel John O'Sullivan, Edward Burke,
and Neil MacEachain.

In Corodale, Charles could only await the return of his messengers. Apart from the primitive nature of the accommodation, he had an idyllic time with perfect sunshine in a magnificent coastal location in the mountains.

Despite friends warning him that sunbathing would bring on a headache, he spent many hours sitting on a stone at the cottage doorway, looking out across the Minch. All the passing ships were the Royal Navy on patrol, but he was convinced that some were French. However, he was never able to persuade MacEachain to sail out to them.

During walks along the shore, Charles

plover. Some gather'd about him, of which he shot two on wing and two on ground. Lachline [*sic*] Dremstill said the art behoove to be witchcraft, for if it was not so the plovers woud conveen to his whistling as to his highness's. Dremstill takes the fewsee and falls a whistling, but tho' he stood there yet no plovers came to his relief. The Prince a second time takes the feuzee, whistles and gathers a croud of the plovers about, and shot a good many.'

Charles continued to have periodic fits of depression, for which he sought comfort in alcohol. Every night, he had only three or four hours sleep, after which he began each day with 'a hearty bumper of brandy' on top of a 'chopin of water which he never failed to drink off at a draught'. He drank heavily at other times also. Some days, he would drink a whole bottle, 'without being in the least concerned'. There was also another mysterious liquid in a pouch, from which he drank 'many drops every morning and throughout the day'. Charles obviously believed that his liquid was a panacea. He insisted that Ned took this liquid to cure a bout of cholic, and 'gae him sae mony draps out o' the little bottlie and Ned soon was as well as ever he had been'.

With this support of alcohol and mild drugs, Charles always managed to appear outwardly in good spirits. At times, he was the life and soul of the party, and 'danced for a whole hour together, having no other musick but some highland reel which he whistled away as he tripped along'.

Physically, he was still troubled by dysentery. The diarrhoea 'kept him very busie'. It also made him feel ill and look pale. O'Sullivan was extremely worried

about it, and suggested various remedies.

'Ah,' says the Prince, 'If I had traicle, I'd be cured imediatly.'

Fortunately, O'Sullivan found a small pot, and, after three days of treacle mixed with broth, Charles was better. The original cause of the condition was thought to be milk, which Charles avoided thereafter.

Throughout this time, MacEachain went on regular sorties to gather news. In addition to daily reports, Boisdale also sent him news from Lady Margaret MacDonald about happenings on the mainland. Although her husband, Sir Alexander MacDonald, was openly supporting Cumberland, she was determined to help Charles.

Much of the information Charles received from the mainland was false. For example, he was told that the clansmen were still in revolt, that Barrisdale had mustered a force of three thousand men at Loch Quoich, and that Cluny had beaten Hanoverian troops at an encounter in Badenoch. Unfortunately, Charles got carried away by these reports, and obdurately tried to convince his companions that all this news heralded an invasion of England by his brother with ten thousand French troops.

Old Clanranald continued to supply Charles with the necessaries of life. He even sent his cook to Corodale, and made several visits himself. Through him, Lady Clanranald sent a complete suit of tartan clothes, comprising a short coat, vest, philibeg, hose, brogues and overcoat. Charles proudly put these on in Old Clanranald's presence.

'Now', says he leping, 'I only the want the Itch to be a compleat Highlander.'

Several times, Old Clanranald and his friends warned Charles that the soldiers, currently rampaging through Moidart, would soon come to scour the Outer Isles.

However, Charles would not be persuaded to leave, despite the obvious danger of being trapped on a small island. In the face of this obstinacy, Old Clanranald and his friends did not press the point, in case Charles suspected that they really wanted him to leave for their own safety, rather than his.

One day, an urchin accidentally wandered to the cottage, and began to handle some meat that Ned Burke was cutting up into collops. When Ned gave the boy a cuff with the back of his hand, Charles immediately remonstrated.

'O man, you don't remember the Scripture which commands to feed the hungry and cleed the naked etc. You ought rather to give him the meat than a strip.'

Charles ordered that the boy be fed, and given some old clothes.

'I cannot see a Christian perish for want of food and raiment had I the power to support them.'

A few days later, the boy told some government troops that Charles was at Corodale. Fortunately, they refused to believe the boy, and ridiculed his story.

Charles was delighted to welcome Donald MacLeod and Allan MacDonald as they arrived with the brandy, letters and news. A few days later, James MacDonald returned. He had been unable to deliver his letter, because Murray of Broughton had left the head of Loch Arkaig.

The letters from Murray of Broughton and Lochiel told Charles that the clans had disbanded, and many of them had surrendered. He was appalled to read about the atrocities that the Hanoverians were committing. However, he was cheered by Donald MacLeod's news of the impending arrival of the French ship to pick up Lynch at Loch Broom.

A few days later, the sudden appearance of a stranger out of a mist caused great consternation. While Charles ran into the cottage to avoid recognition, O'Sullivan went to meet the newcomer. He introduced himself as Hugh MacDonald of Baleshare, bringing a letter to Charles from Lady Margaret MacDonald. Fortunately, Baleshare was recognised by Allan MacDonald, and was conducted to Charles.

Lady Margaret's letter informed Charles that troops had been sent to both ends of the Outer Isles with the intention of searching their whole length. Baleshare had learned the whereabouts of Charles' hiding place from Boisdale. As Boisdale himself wanted to tell Charles about the Skye militia landing on Barra, they both decided to go independently to Corodale by different routes.

To Baleshare, the royal personage cut a very strange figure. For the audience, Charles wore his nightcap. In addition, his clothes, hands and face were smeared with soot. However, Charles was not in the least embarrassed about his appearance, and immediately welcomed Baleshare with a dram. They were also served with a leg of beef, together with half a stone of butter on a wooden plate. Soon afterwards, Boisdale arrived, and was greeted by Charles with all the usual warmth and enthusiasm reserved for old drinking friends. When Baleshare and Boisdale told Charles their news, he showed little concern, because the troops landing on Barra were MacDonalds and MacLeods. He believed that, out of their fundamental loyalty to him, they would not search very diligently.

Charles then discussed with Boisdale and Baleshare the problem of his escaping from South Uist, and making his way to Loch Broom to meet the rescue ship. Baleshare proposed that, as soon as Boisdale found a boat, Charles should first cross the Minch to Fladda-chuain, a remote island off the north coast of the

Trotternish peninsula on Skye. He assured Charles, that Lady Margaret would be able and willing to help him escape from there to the mainland. Baleshare undertook to inform Lady Margaret of the plan. Through Baleshare, Charles sent her a letter, 'thanking her for the kindness in sending him the newspapers, that he was very sensible of her favours and hoped she would continue them'.

When business was done, Charles insisted that Boisdale and Baleshare should both stay the night, and enjoy themselves. As soon as Boisdale had been shaved by Ned Burke, and put on a clean shirt, the drinking began. For a while, they all retained sufficient of their faculties to discuss politics, and exchange frank opinions.

Baleshare became bold enough to tell Charles that the greatest objections to his acceptance in Britain were his Catholic religion, and a fear that he might exercise an arbitrary style of government. In reply, Charles argued that these were two misrepresentations put about by his enemies.

Boisdale said that there was also another fear that Charles might forget the Highlanders as soon as they restored him to the throne. He told Charles that King Charles II, some eighty years previously, had certainly let the Highlanders down in this way. In particular, Boisdale's own ancestor, Donald Clanranald, had fought seven battles on behalf of Charles II, only to be disowned later at the king's court. However, Charles assured Boisdale that such things would not happen again.

'Boystill, Dont be rubbing up old sores, for if I cam home the case woud be otherwise with me.'

Eventually, the party degenerated into carousing,` and the drinking lasted three days and nights. By all accounts, Charles had the better of them all, even surpassing Boisdale, who had great notoriety for his drinking prowess.

The revelry ended with the return of MacEachain from one of his forays to seek information. He revealed that the troops had been informed that Charles was hiding in the area. He also confirmed everything that Baleshare and Boisdale had told Charles.

Somehow, MacEachain very quickly brought them all to their senses. At last, Charles came to realise the seriousness of his position. It now seemed impossible either to escape or avoid capture. For the first time, Charles openly showed dejection. Boisdale, however, believed that the danger was not so great, and was confident that he could find a place to hide Charles until it was easier to escape. Meanwhile, he persuaded Charles to move north, away from the troops, to the deserted island of Ouia, just off the south-east coast of Benbecula. He then took his leave in order to make the other arrangements. At eleven o' clock on 5 June, Charles set sail for Ouia with MacEachain, O'Sullivan, Ned Burke, and Donald MacLeod.

7
5 - 15 JUNE
SOUTH UIST to BENBECULA

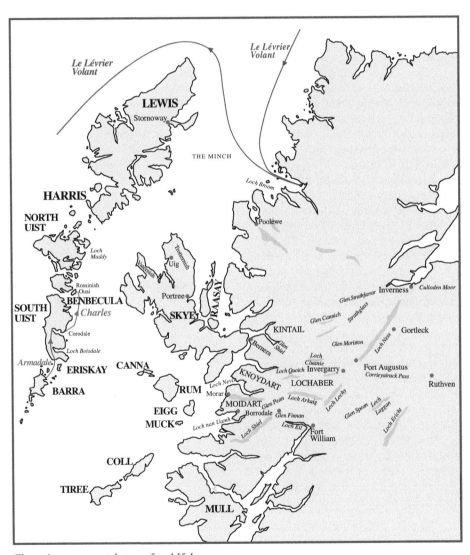

The various movements between 5 and 15 June

The Enemy

At sea, Captain Noel had now been replaced as commanding naval officer by Commodore Thomas Smith, who had brought more ships to the Minch. Smith and Campbell planned to investigate a report that Charles had escaped to the distant island of St Kilda. Meanwhile, the other ships kept close watch on the Irish meal ship. In the Outer Isles, the build-up of government troops continued. On 14 July, the Skye militia swarmed on to South Uist from Barra.

At Tobermory on Mull, Aeneas Macdonald, one of the original 'Seven Men of Moidart' was brought before General Campbell. On the mainland, Fergussone captured Lord Lovat on an island in Loch Morar. Under questioning, both men revealed that Charles was now in Uist. Further inland, Barrisdale turned traitor. Giving himself up to Lord Loudoun, he offered to provide information, and try to capture Charles. In exchange, he wanted his personal freedom, and the security of his property. Although this deal was made in secret, news of it quickly leaked out.

The Friends

Lochiel From the island on Loch Shiel, Lochiel and Murray of Broughton made their circuitous way by boat and horseback to Appin. After a fruitless wait of several days for Charles' reply to their letter, they parted company. Murray travelled south.

MacDonald of Armadale Armadale now realised that he had an opportunity to help Charles. Suspecting that Boisdale and Old Clanranald would know exactly where Charles was hiding, Armadale hoped to make contact with Charles through them. He informed Boisdale in advance of all the troop movements so that Charles could be warned.

O'Neil When O'Neil and Lady Clanranald returned to Nunton, they learned that Old Clanranald had recently left for Fort Augustus in response to a summons by Cumberland. They also received a visit from Armadale's 23-year-old stepdaughter, Flora, who had just sailed over from Skye. She was en route to Milton to visit her brother, Angus, and his wife, Penelope, who was Clanranald's daughter. During this visit, she and O'Neil talked about the Prince. O'Neil asked whether she would like to see Charles. 'She reply'd that as she had not had that happiness before, she did not look for it now, but that a sight of him wou'd make her happy, tho' he was on a hill and she on another.'

The French The third rescue mission in *Le Hardi Mendiant* set off from Dunkirk on 10 June. Once again, her commander was Mathieu Dumont.

The first rescue mission in *Le Lévrier Volant* anchored in Loch Broom on 11 June. Fortunately, no government troops had reached so far north at that time. The ship was able to remain there unmolested. However, the local minister, Rev. James Robertson, was a staunch Hanoverian . Moreover, he sent regular reports to Cumberland at Fort Augustus.

The officers of *Le Lévrier Volant* soon made contact with MacKenzie of Ardloch, who, after serving as a captain in Charles' army at Culloden, had returned to his family home at Loch Broom. Ardloch warned the Frenchmen that the local minister would certainly inform Cumberland of their arrival. Ardloch's wife introduced them to Captain Lynch, who was now in the area, waiting for the ship to take him back to France. Lynch advised Dumay to look for Charles in the Outer Isles. *Le Lévrier Volant* therefore set sail immediately. While cruising down the west coast of the Outer Isles, the sloop was chased by two ships of the Royal Navy. Eventually, Dumay decided to head back to France.

The Prince

The Prince's companions: Colonel John O'Sullivan, Edward Burke, Donald MacLeod, and Neil MacEachain.

Charles and his friends arrived safely at Ouia, and sent notice of their arrival to Nunton. They were soon re-joined by O'Neil, and visited by Lady Clanranald, who came with provisions.

From Kilbride, Boisdale kept in regular contact with Charles, and arranged for supplies to be delivered. After about three days, Boisdale, acting on Armadale's tip-off, informed Charles that Ouia was about to be searched. He advised Charles to cross over to Benbecula, and go to a remote area of Rossinish. Accordingly, Charles and MacEachain trekked all round Loch Uiskevagh, and found an isolated shieling.

Back on Ouia, there was great consternation when the island was visited by MacLeod of Hamara, 'a great villain', who was known to be no friend of Charles' cause. He claimed to be looking for MacEachain. When Charles' friends told MacLeod that MacEachain had gone to see Clanranald, he left, much to everyone's great relief.

O'Sullivan kept in contact with Charles using the boat. After two days, he brought Charles a message from Boisdale with the news that a detachment of MacLeods was now marching north to search the whole of Benbecula. The message urged Charles to move to Loch Eynort. In reply, Charles explained that his departure had to be delayed, because the wind was blowing in the wrong direction for him to sail there.

Also, the boats of the militia were searching Loch Uiskevagh. The very next day, Boisdale sent a message saying 'yt he must come at any reat'. Fortunately, the friends remaining on Ouia were able to row across to Rossinish that night. Charles and all his friends then set off, sailing south along the coast.

Loch Uiskevagh

Ouia from Peter's Port,
Benbecula

8
15 - 21 JUNE
BENBECULA to SOUTH UIST

The various movements between 15 and 21 June

The Enemy

On 15 June, the *Raven* and the *Baltimore* sailed into Loch Boisdale to seek intelligence. Thirty soldiers immediately went to Kilbride, and brought Boisdale from his house. He was detained for questioning on board the *Baltimore*.

The next day, HMS *Trial* reached Barra with a company commanded by Captain Caroline Scott, an officer who had recently behaved with the most despicable cruelty in searching for rebels in Lochaber and Appin. A few days later, Scott and his troops crossed to South Uist, landing at Kilbride.

Meanwhile, the Skye militia had gradually worked their way up South Uist. They advanced northwards five or six miles a day, scouring every inch from coast to coast. The plan now was that they would soon return south to meet Scott. In this way, they were certain that they must ensnare Charles.

On 19 June, Campbell set off to St Kilda with the *Furnace* and the *Terror*. On the way, they were joined by a flottila commanded by Commodore Smith. As soon as they arrived at St Kilda, they realised they had been on a wild-goose chase. Campbell set off back to the Outer Isles, while Smith headed for Barra.

The Friends

Lochiel After staying a few days at Appin, Lochiel, with his surgeon, Sir Stuart Threpland, sailed up Loch Leven, and made his way across Rannoch Moor to Loch Treig. Here, he met Cluny and Cluny's brother-in-law, Young MacPherson of Breakachie. Soon, they were joined by Archibald Cameron and Rev. John Cameron.

They then all moved to a remote bothy deep in Badenoch. There, they adopted a very strict regime of security. Only close personal family, friends, and servants knew their whereabouts. Nobody was allowed to come to them unless on their orders, or with their agreement. Such meetings were always arranged through Young Breakachie. Cluny also had his clansmen keeping watch on troop movements in the area.

MacDonald of Armadale As Armadale led the Skye militia northwards, he drew up a scheme for Charles' escape. The plan was that Charles would disguise himself as a lady's maid, who would sail to Skye with her mistress on a journey authorised by Armadale himself. The mistress was to be Armadale's stepdaughter, Flora, who was now at Milton. The pretext for Flora's journey was to be that she was returning home to her mother on Skye.

Knowing that the Skye militia would soon be moving south, Armadale realised that Charles had now very little chance of avoiding capture. He therefore sent Charles a message through Lady Clanranald, advising him of the great danger, and proposing the plan of escape. He also informed Charles where Flora might be found.

The Prince

The Prince's companions: Colonel John O'Sullivan, Captain Felix O'Neil, Edward Burke, Donald MacLeod, and Neil MacEachain.

Over several days, Charles and his friends made their way to Loch Boisdale by boat. They did the journey in stages, stopping off at various places, such as Corodale, on the way.

At daybreak on the morning after leaving Loch Uiskevagh, they were off the coast of Ornish, where they were surprised by the sudden appearance of the *Baltimore* and the *Raven*. Charles' crew immediately made for a narrow inlet, Acasaid Fhalaich, on the shore. To their horror, one of the enemy sloops sent a boat towards the inlet. Although they

Arcasaid Fhalaich

were convinced that they had been discovered, Charles and his friends could do nothing. Fortunately, the boat was only collecting fresh water from a nearby spring. With this mission accomplished, the sloops went on their way. However, as there were other ships in the vicinity, the fugitives decided to stay put. They endured misery throughout the night and the following day.

> 'It rained cruelle, there was not a house within a mil of us, no shelter but a Rock, when the thyd was out, we got under rocks where we got some heather, tho'wet, we made use of it; we durst not set up our seal for fear of being seen from the mountains. When the thyed came in wer were obliged to retir, & be exposed all night long to the rains.'

Off the island of Stuley, they sighted an object that looked like another enemy ship.

The estuary opposite Kyle Stuley

As a precaution, they took refuge in Kyle Stuley, the channel between the island and the mainland. With lookouts placed on the mainland at distances of a mile or more from their landing place, it was safe enough to sleep in an improvised tent made from the boat's sail and oars. Charles rested in the tent on a bed of heather, while MacEachain went to seek food.

MacEachain returned with milk. He also had news that troops from the Skye militia had already searched that area two days ago.

At night, the fugitives completed the final leg to Loch Boisdale, landing on the island of Calvay. Immediately, they lit a fire in the ruin of an old tower, and put on their cooking pot. Ned Burke prepared Charles' bed of heather.

Early next morning, MacEachain walked the three miles to Boisdale's house, where he found everyone asleep. On waking them up, MacEachain heard about Boisdale's detention. Boisdale's wife supplied MacEachain with butter, cheese and brandy. She also agreed to try and find out what the troops were doing.

Back on Calvay, Charles, who had not eaten since leaving Rossinish, fell upon the food.

'Come, come,' said he, 'give me one of the bottles and a piece of the bread, for I was never so hungry since I was born.'

They were all dismayed about Boisdale's detention. However, as Boisdale had never overtly come out for Charles during the rebellion, everyone thought he might be released soon. Nevertheless, Boisdale's detention was a great blow. With Old Clanranald away on the mainland, Boisdale had been Charles' only source of help.

The rain poured incessantly. Charles suffered badly from midges, and, because of his continual scratching, the many cuts and grazes on his legs became infected.

The friends discussed their predicament endlessly. One suggestion was that they should make a break for the mainland in the small boat. Another idea was to go to Barra, and hide on one of its smaller islands, that had already been searched by the troops. This latter plan was immediately abandoned when Lady Boisdale sent a message announcing Scott's landing on Barra.

Two sloops appeared, and stationed themselves at the mouth of Loch Boisdale. As a precaution, the boatmen moved Charles' boat further up the loch, while Charles, together with O'Neil, O'Sullivan and MacEachain, landed on the north bank. From there, they could escape to the hills if Scott's troops should come north to Loch Boisdale. In fact, Charles and his friends spent the rest of the day in a cave behind Beinn Ruigh Choinnich.

With the exit from the loch blocked by the sloops, and the prospect of Scott's troops marching up from the south, Charles realised

Loch Boisdale and Calvay

that they would be completely surrounded, if the Skye militia should now come back from the north. Charles therefore sent two messengers to find out the troop movements at each end of South Uist. Rory MacDonald was sent to Kilbride, and his brother, John, set off to the north.

> 'Yu may believe yt those were critical moments, but there was no remedy, but to rely on providence.'

That night, Charles and his friends returned across Loch Boisdale to the south bank in order to be nearer Lady Boisdale, their only source of information. They slept in the makeshift tent. Being too conspicuous during the day, it was dismantled early in the morning.

The next day, the two sloops sailed away. Spirits were boosted with news of Boisdale's impending release at Barra. However, they were dashed almost immediately, when Fergussone re-arrested him on the journey from Barra to South Uist. There were also alarming reports of seven men-of-war in the straits between Barra and South Uist. Charles' worst fears were confirmed when John MacDonald returned with news that the Skye militia had been ordered to come south from Benbecula. Round about the same time, Charles received the messenger bearing Armadale's letter with the plan of escape.

After another night in the open, Rory Macdonald came running early in the morning with the news that Scott's troops had now landed at Kilbride. He also reported that Boisdale's house had been ransacked. Furthermore, Lady Boisdale, together with her stepdaughter and servants, had been tied neck-and-heel during a brutal interrogation. Rory was also convinced that Scott now knew where Charles was.

In the immediate panic, nobody knew what to do.

> 'All choices were bad, but (under God) they behoved to remove from the place where they then were, and to do their best.'

Everyone set about packing the boat. Just as they were about to leave, Charles noticed that a quarter of mutton and a bowl of meal, had been abandoned on the camp site.

The cave behind Beinn Ruigh Choinnich

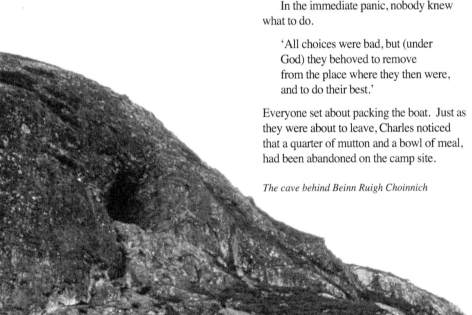

'A Gad,' says the Prince, 'they shall never say yt we were so pressed, yt we abandoned our meat.'

With great coolness, he retrieved the food. At that moment, they heard musket shots. Looking up the hill behind them, they saw what seemed to be a hundred soldiers. The fugitives immediately clambered aboard their boat, and rowed into the creeks among the islands at the head of Loch Boisdale. There, they stopped to look back. Although there was no sign of any pursuers, they were horrified to see the *Baltimore* and *Raven* reappearing at the entrance to the loch. Charles and his friends then completed the crossing of the loch. One of the men ran up a hill, and, on returning, confirmed that no boats had set out after them. For the moment, at least, they seemed to be safe.

This narrow escape now convinced Charles he would certainly be caught if he stayed in the Outer Isles. In the absence of any other plan, he decided to go to Benbecula, and try Armadale's escape plan. As the Skye militia would be making their way down from Benbecula, their route northwards had to be over the high ground in order to avoid meeting them. In addition, Charles decided that the only way to make the journey safely was by moving quickly with just two companions. O'Neil was chosen, because, unlike 'O'Sullivan, he was physically fit. MacEachain was chosen to be their guide. When Charles announced his decision to break up the party, there was a general outcry of dismay from his companions. O'Sullivan was particularly distraught.

'I have followed yu until now, & it is not in the most critical & dangerouse moment, yt Il quit yu, what wou'd the world think of it?'

Charles replied, 'Never mind what the world thinks, no body knows better then I

do, the services yu have rendred me, & no body can suspect your fidelity & attachemt after the proofs yu have given me of them.'

Charles went on to outline Armadale's escape plan, and asked O'Sullivan to bring the boat up to Benbecula, so that they could use it to sail to Skye. He also explained that he was going to hide in the cave behind Beinn Ruigh Choinnich, until he was sure what the Skye militia were doing. He asked O'Sullivan to stay with the boatmen, and pay them 'a shilling sterling a day, besides their maintenance'. If, by some mischance, O'Sullivan did not meet up with Charles at Benbecula, he was to make his own way to France, and report to Charles' brother.

> 'Sullivan cant containe, he burst out a crying to quit the Prince & to see the danger & misery he was exposed to; the Prince embrasses him & holds him in his arms for a quarter of an hour, Sullivan talking to him as much as his tears & sobs cou'd permit him.'

As Charles set off, all the boatmen began to 'cry & roar'. At the sound of their sobs, Charles walked back. He assured them that they would hear from him that night or the next day, when O'Neil would come down to collect some bread that Charles had asked O'Sullivan to bake. For a parting shot, he called, 'We will all joyn again.'
'

9
21 - 24 JUNE
SOUTH UIST to BENBECULA

21 - 22 June

The Enemy

Despite Charles' fears, the troops did not know where he was. The troops that ransacked Kilbride were searching for arms and Spanish gold, that might have been hidden there. The shots, that Charles had heard, were fired by soldiers wantonly killing cattle. At night, the troops re-embarked for Barra, while the two sloops, that had arrived at the entrance to the loch, went off without even dropping anchor.

Having returned from St Kilda, Campbell landed a large force for a brief search of Pabbay, a small island off the west coast of North Uist. They went on to the neighbouring island of Berneray, from where General Campbell intended to sweep down North Uist, Benbecula, and South Uist.

By this time, the Skye militia had reached the narrow straits separating South Uist from Benbecula. There, Armadale set up a cordon to guard access to the ford. The sentries were stationed within gunshot distance of each other right across the north coast of South Uist.

The Friends

Anguier *Le Bien Trouvé* anchored in Loch Broom in the morning of 21 June, and immediately sent a longboat ashore. The crew soon made contact with the local MacKenzies, who were unable to tell them where Charles might be found. However, they warned the Frenchmen that the local minister, Rev. James Robertson, would certainly inform Cumberland of their arrival. They advised

Anguier to leave immediately, and land further south at Loch Ewe. Accordingly, the ship set sail the same day with a local pilot aboard.

Lady Margaret MacDonald On Skye, the letter Charles wrote to Lady Margaret from Corodale was delivered by Baleshare's brother, Donald Roy MacDonald, who lived very close to her. Donald Roy also showed her a letter from Baleshare informing him of Charles' plan to sail from South Uist to Fladda-chuain, and asking him to supply Charles with shirts and blankets.

As soon as they had read both letters, Donald Roy suggested that they should both follow Baleshare's instructions by burning them. However, Lady Margaret refused, and, kissing her letter, said, 'No, I will not burn it, I will preserve it for the sake of him who writ it to me. Although King George's forces should come to the house, I hope I shall find a way to secure the letter.' While Donald Roy set fire to his letter, she put hers in a cupboard.

She then asked Donald Roy to go and reonnoitre Fladda-chuain in preparation for Charles' arrival. Meanwhile, she arranged for six of Sir Alexander's shirts to be washed ready for delivery to Charles. She also sent twenty guineas, which her servants changed into small coins

The Prince

The Prince's companions: Captain Felix O'Neil and Neil MacEachain.

In the cave behind Beinn Ruigh Choinnich, Charles, O'Neil and MacEachain waited for darkness. During the day, a messenger from O'Sullivan brought four

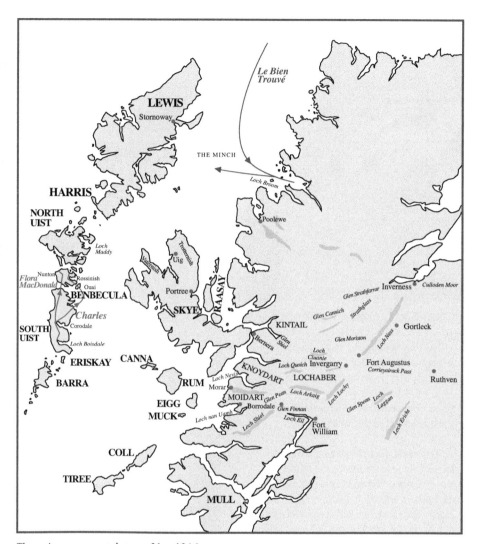

The various movements between 21 and 24 June

cakes, some boiled mutton and some water.

Having decided to join in with Armadale's escape plan, Charles wanted to meet Flora MacDonald, and ask her to play her crucial part. Knowing that she was currently tending her brother's cattle at Alisary, a remote grazing ground in the hills above the southern shore of Loch Eynort, MacEachain agreed to take Charles there on the way to Benbecula.

After a meal of bread and cheese, they all set off in the late evening. Each man carried some baggage, but MacEachain also carried the provisions, his own gun and sword, as well as one of Charles' fusees in its holster. Charles was very impressed with MacEachain.

Flora MacDonald's grazing land at Alisary

'As they were going on, the prince clapt Neil's shoulder, often telling him if ever it was their good fortune to get free of their present troubles, he would make him live easie all his days for the fatigue of that night.'

Flora MacDonald

That night, Flora MacDonald was sleeping alone in a bothy on the family's grazing ground. When Charles, O'Neil and MacEachain arrived, it was midnight. While Charles and O'Neil waited at some distance from the bothy, MacEachain, who knew Flora well, went on to wake her. A few minutes later, O'Neil went to join them. At first, O'Neil pretended that the purpose of this visit was to find out when the Skye militia would be passing through Alisary on the way south. Eventually, he announced that he had 'brought a friend to see her'. From her previous meeting with O'Neil at Nunton, Flora knew that he was one of Charles' close friends. She therefore guessed who this 'friend' might be, With 'some emotion', she asked if it was the Prince. On hearing O'Neil's reply, she dashed out of the bothy, even though 'she got scarcely on the half of her close'. Inviting Charles into the bothy, 'she brought to him a part of the best cheer she had', including a large bowl full of cream. After two or three gulps, Charles passed it on to his companions, who finished it off.

It was not long before Charles told Flora of the escape plan, and asked her to play the part that her stepfather had designed for her. However, her immediate response was to decline. In addition to a natural fear for the hazards and dangers that she would have to endure, she was concerned that Sir Alexander MacDonald, a long-time friend of her family, would be ruined, if the plot were discovered. She was also worried about 'the risque she would run of losing her character in a malicious and ill-natured world'.

O'Neil then began persuading her to change her mind. He emphasised 'the honour and immortality that would redound to her by such a glorious action', and 'was at some pains to represent to her the glory and honour she would acquire by such a worthy and heroic action'. O'Neil assured her that Sir Alexander, being on the mainland at that time, could not be implicated. O'Neil's solution to her final worry was quite drastic!

'But if you will still entertain fears about your character, I shall (by an oath) marry you directly, if you please.'

Eventually, Flora agreed to take part in the plot, but without accepting the offer of marriage. She then left for her brother's house at Milton. She intended to travel on that same day to Benbecula, where she would meet her stepfather and Lady Clanranald at Nunton. Flora promised to send a message to Charles later that day with more details of the plan. Meanwhile, MacEachain told her that he, together with Charles and O'Neil, would wait in a cave on Hecla, a mountain just a few miles to the north.

Hecla (on left)
and Ben Corodale (on right)

On the way to Hecla, the three men passed close by Howbeg, MacEachain's birthplace. Here, they learned of General Campbell's troops landing in North Uist. By the time they reached the cave, it was sunrise. Charles was exhausted and hungry. After eating some bread and cheese, that Flora had given them, Charles slept, while O'Neil and MacEachain took turns to stand guard. Later, MacEachain went off to find food, and returned with 'abundance of such cheer as the neighbourhood could afford'.

As the day drew on, Charles became impatient to hear from Flora. By eight o'clock in the evening, he could wait no longer, and decided to send MacEachain to obtain news from her. Despite MacEachain's weariness, Charles ordered him to make the 25-mile return journey to Nunton by four o'clock the next afternoon.

The cave on Hecla

22 - 23 June

The Friends

Flora MacDonald Having reached the ford over the straits from South Uist to Benbecula, Flora had run into difficulties. She had been arrested by the Skye militia, because she did not have a pass to make the crossing. Fortunately, she had the presence

of mind and the *savoir faire* to ask who was the commanding officer of these troops. On learning that is was none other than her stepfather, she refused to answer any questions until she was taken to him. She was therefore taken to his command post on the other side of the ford. There, she told Armadale of her intention to take part in his plan. He then gave her a pass to sail to Skye with Neil MacEachain, and her maid, 'Betty Burke'.

In order to add an extra touch of authenticity, Armadale wrote a letter for her to deliver to her mother.

> ' I have sent your daughter from this
> country lest she should be any
> way frightened with the troops lying
> here. She has got one Bettie
> Burk, an Irish girl, who as she tells
> me is a good spinster. If her
> spinning pleases you, you may keep
> her till she spin all your lint;
> or if you have any wool to spin you
> may employ her.'

(22 June, 1746)

MacEachain By the time Neil reached the ford over to Benbecula, it was late at night. Like Flora, he was immediately apprehended by the Skye militia. Next morning, he was taken for questioning by Armadale. At Armadale's command post, he met Flora having breakfast with her stepfather and some other men. In a private conversation, Flora explained that, because of her detention by the troops, she had not yet met Lady Clanranald. However, she was going to leave for Nunton in half an hour. It was then arranged that MacEachain would take Charles and O'Neil to Rossinish, where Flora and Lady Clanranald would be waiting in the bothy that Charles and his friends used when they first landed on Benbecula. Soon afterwards, MacEachain was released, and set off back to Charles with the news.

The Prince

The Prince's companions:
Captain Felix O'Neil, and Neil MacEachain.

At the cave on Hecla, O'Neil was showing the signs of strain caused by the days of continual tension and anxiety. He was now totally demoralised and depressed. He was so convinced they would be captured, that he temporarily persuaded Charles that they should surrender to General Campbell. However, Charles' nerve soon revived.

'O'Neil, is this all the faith and trust you have in God? Let us only take care to have enough of faith and trust in his providence and there is no fear of us at all. Pull up your spirits, man. Never despair.'

Hoping to take O'Neil's mind off his woes, Charles led his companion on a foray to find some food. At an isolated cottage, an old woman gave them eggs and bear-bannocks. She also pointed to a nearby hill, where, she said, there were two girls who would milk their goats to give Charles and O'Neil a drink. While Charles bounded nimbly up towards them, O'Neil trudged wearily behind. On reaching the girls, O'Neil slumped miserably to the grass. As all Charles' urgings to revive him were unsuccessful, Charles, in desperation, turned to girls for help.

'Come my lasses, what would you think to dance a Highland reel with me? We cannot have a bagpipe just now, but I shall sing you a Strathspey reel.'

Charles then proceeded to skip, knacking his thumbs and clapping his hands to the rhythm. Eventually, O'Neil, realising that this frolic was only to cheer him up, was shamed out of his torpor.

Later, they returned to the cave, where MacEachain arrived in the evening. On hearing of MacEachain's meeting with Flora, and the plan for them all to meet at Rossinish, Charles decided that they should leave

immediately. As the ford over to Benbecula was closely guarded, a crossing on foot was impossible. They therefore had to travel by boat during the night. MacEachain thought that they could obtain a boat quickly at Loch Skiport, just at the foot of the northern slopes of Hecla. They began the descent towards the loch in darkness.

23 - 24 June

The Friends

Immediately she arrived at Nunton, Flora began making arrangements with Lady Clanranald for Charles' escape to Skye. They sent messages to summon some boatmen, and started to make arrangements for the dress for 'Betty Burke'.

The dress had to look authentic for an Irish peasant girl. It also had to fit a six-foot man. As such, a dress could not be found 'off the peg', Flora and Lady Clanranald had to design it, and make it specially. Moreover, it would take several days to sew.

'The gown was of caligo, a light coloured quilted petticlat, a mantle of dun camlet made after the Irish fashion with a cap to cover his royal highness whole head and face, with a suitable head-dress, shoes, stockings, etc.'

The Prince

The Prince's companions: Captain Felix O'Neil and Neil MacEachain.

On reaching the shore of Loch Skiport, Charles and his friends met four men who had come to the loch several days previously to fish. As MacEachain knew the men well, they were immediately engaged to take Charles, O'Neil and MacEachain in their yawl to Ouia, where

Loch Skiport

MacEachain expected to find a friend, Ranald MacDonald. The yawl covered the five miles while it was still dark. On finding that MacDonald was not there, MacEachain ordered the boatmen to sail the boat across the narrow straits to Benbecula, so that he, Charles and O'Neil could continue to Rossinish on foot. On landing their passengers on a rocky promontory, the boatmen were paid, and dismissed.

Looking north from Ouia

Charles and O'Neil then fell asleep, while MacEachain went to explore the surroundings. No sooner had he walked ten yards, MacEachain saw, to his horror, that instead of landing on the mainland, they were actually on an island separated from the mainland by a wide channel. He went back to report the matter to Charles, who immediately went into a rage. In his ranting, Charles blamed MacEachain for this misfortune, and showered curses on the boatmen who, he said, had deliberately brought them to the island so that he would starve with hunger and cold. To make matters worse, it was now raining hard. MacEachain did his best to pacify Charles, by offering to swim across the channel, and bring a boat. However, as he was undressing, he noticed that the outgoing tide had just revealed a rock previously submerged in the middle of the channel. Knowing that the tide would retreat much further, MacEachain persuaded Charles to let him delay his departure to see if they could eventually walk over to the other side. After three quarters of an hour, they were able to do so.

This was the second time in two weeks that Charles had begun to walk across the moor to Rossinish. However, this time the weather was foul. The three men were soon soaked to the skin, and numb with cold. Charles was also faint through lack of food. After quarter of a mile, they came across two shielings from which two men approached them. MacEachain told the two men, who were Clanranald's tenants, that his companions were Irish gentlemen escaping from Culloden. He also persuaded them to provide shelter and refreshment. Charles and his friends then 'feasted splendidly upon such cheer as there was to be had'.

Later, they were guided across the rest of the moor by a young boy, whom they hired for half a guinea. Round about five in the afternoon, they stopped to rest by the side of a loch, where Charles shivered continuously with cold. When they set off again, it was so dark that they could not see three yards ahead. In addition, the rain poured, and a gale blew. Charles frequently stumbled into peat hags, often losing his shoes. MacEachain had to retrieve them by fishing in the bog with his arm buried up to the shoulder.

On nearing the bothy, that was their destination, MacEachain left Charles and O'Neil some distance away, while he went on alone. From the occupants, a man and wife, he discovered that Flora MacDonald and Lady Clanranald had not yet arrived. However, he was more alarmed to learn that twenty Skye militia were camped just quarter of a mile away. Charles was so exasperated when MacEachain reported this fact that he 'was like to tear his clothes to pieces'. Fortunately, their guide knew that they could stay safely four miles away at the house of one of Clanranald's boomen. He therefore led them to it.

They had hardly rested before Charles resolved to send MacEachain immediately to tell Flora and Lady Clanranald of his arrival. However, MacEachain was reluctant to leave Charles, because, in the event of a surprise appearance by the enemy, only he knew where to go for safety. Charles sent O'Neil on the mission, accompanied by their guide.

10
24 - 29 JUNE
BENBECULA to SKYE

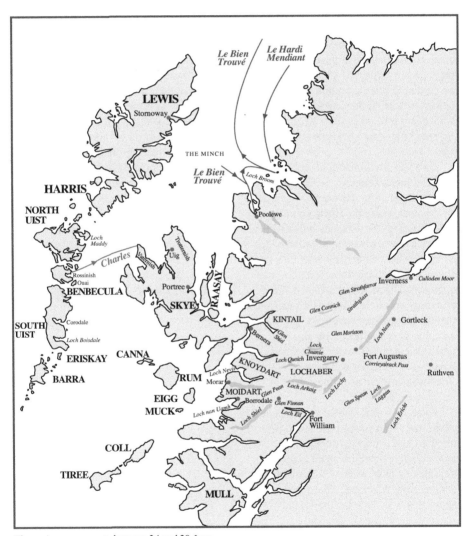

The various movements between 24 and 29 June

The Friends

Anguier Having retreated from Loch Broom, and spent a few days in the open sea, *Le Bien Trouvé* anchored in Loch Ewe in the evening of 26 June. Although several Jacobite fugitives were there, none could give reliable information about Charles' whereabouts. They could only suggest that Anguier should contact Murray of Broughton, who, they thought, was still at Loch Arkaig.

The locals also warned Anguier that the Royal Navy's sloops frequently visited the loch, and that it was too dangerous for his ship to stay inshore. They advised him to leave a few men to try and find Charles, while the ship cruised in the relative safety of the open sea. One of the locals, MacKenzie of Gruinard, told them that Charles' former aide-de-camp, Alexander MacLeod, would arrive at Loch Ewe any day. As Macleod had recently been with Charles at Loch Arkaig. MacKenzie thought that MacLeod would be able to give them some reliable information. Gruinard then offered to introduce them to Alexander MacLeod, when he arrived.

Flora MacDonald Flora and Lady Clanranald were beginning to have second thoughts about the wisdom of the proposed adventure. They were worried that, with so many ships patrolling the Minch, any boat sailing between Benbecula and Skye would be intercepted. They thought that Charles would be safer to go to North Uist, where, they believed, Baleshare could hide him indefinitely. They decided to suggest this plan to Baleshare, and to arrange for him to meet Charles.

The Prince

The Prince's companions: Captain Felix O'Neil and Neil MacEachain.

At daybreak on 25 June, the booman's wife told Charles that the militia came to buy milk from them every morning. Charles and MacEachain therefore went to the shore of Loch Uiskevagh, intending to stay there until the militia had been and gone. For three hours, they sat under a rock, trying to shelter from the incessant rain. Unfortunately, the rock was too small to provide adequate cover. They were soon wet through. Despite wrapping himself in his plaid, Charles was tormented by midges. As they swarmed over his face and hands, he uttered 'such hideous cries and complaints as would have rent the rocks with compassion'. From time to time, the booman's dairymaid came with news. It was to Charles' great relief when she reported that it was safe to return.

A large fire was waiting for Charles and MacEachain in the bothy. Immediately they entered, MacEachain set about stripping Charles of his clothes, and hanging them on lines all round the bothy. Charles sat by the fire in his shirt 'as merry and hearty as if he was in the best room at Whitehall'. As soon as he was warm, Charles enquired if there was any food. The booman's wife had some milk, but, despite the fact that she intended it for her children, MacEachain persuaded her to let Charles have it. She warmed it up, and whisked it into a thick solid-looking froth. As she gave the pot to Charles, MacEachain jokingly announced that it contained fresh cream. Whereupon, Charles put aside his spoon, and dipped his hand in the pot as a scoop. As soon as he felt the hot liquid, Charles jerked his hand back in pain. Angrily, he accused the woman of deliberately causing him to be scalded, and launched into a tirade of curses against her. MacEachain, convulsing with laughter, grabbed an oar, and announced that he was going to punish the woman by beating her within an inch of her life. Believing that MacEachain was serious, Charles calmed down immediately. He begged his friend not to touch the woman in case she ran off to bring the soldiers. Later, Charles, wrapped in his wet plaid, went to sleep on an improvised bed made from the bothy door covered with a ragged old sail.

In the evening, the young boy, who had taken O'Neil to Nunton, returned with a roasted fowl and two bottles of wine. Charles 'supp't very heartily', before sleeping that night on a bed made by MacEachain from heather.

The boy also brought a letter in which O'Neil informed Charles of Flora's alternative plan to go to North Uist. The letter also told Charles that O'Neil and Baleshare would like to meet Charles the next day on the summit of Rueval, a nearby hill.

With MacEachain as his guide, Charles went to the meeting place, where Baleshare announced that he would not be able to hide Charles at all. He was worried that his overlord, Sir Alexander MacDonald, would be implicated, if the plan failed. Baleshare was also unwilling to advise Charles what else to do, in case he made Charles' predicament worse. However, Baleshare did say that, if Charles reached Skye, the Laird of MacKinnon, would be sure to arrange a crossing to the mainland. Baleshare also gave Charles the names of other Jacobite sympathisers, including MacDonald of Kingsburgh, who would be able and willing to protect him on Skye.

Loch Uiskevagh

Later in the day, fifty soldiers appeared within half a mile of them. Charles and his friends therefore returned to Rossinish. O'Neil then went back to Nunton with a message from Charles expressing his disappointment at the break-down of the arrangement with Baleshare, and entreating Flora to keep her promise to take him to Skye. He also asked her to come next day, because, with the steady build-up of the enemy troops, there was no time to lose.

Early next morning, two brothers, John and Roderick MacDonald, arrived to inform Charles that both the crew and the boat were ready. Charles decided that MacEachain should fetch Flora from Nunton immediately. Charles and the two MacDonalds walked with MacEachain for some of the way. On parting company, Charles and the two brothers climbed to the top of Rueval, where they could survey the whole countryside for miles around.

The Enemy

Having scoured the whole of North Uist for six days, Campbell's troops moved over to Benbecula on 27 June. On the same day, the *Furnace* transported two hundred redcoats from Barra to reinforce the troops already on Benbecula. Convinced that Charles must be on Benbecula or South Uist, Campbell was confident that his troops' next sweep south would flush out their quarry.

The Friends

Flora MacDonald Now that it was finally decided that Charles was going to Skye, Flora was ready to leave Nunton with Lady Clanranald, O'Neil, and some other members of Lady Clanranald's household. When MacEachain arrived, it was arranged that O'Neil would go alone on foot to warn Charles that Flora was on her way. Meanwhile, MacEachain took the rest of the party to Rossinish by boat.

Mrs Margaret MacDonald of Kirkibost It was decided that Lady Margaret MacDonald, on Skye, should be warned of

Loch Uiskevagh

Charles' impending arrival. Accordingly, Mrs Margaret MacDonald of Kirkibost would take this message to Skye the day before Charles left. Although her husband, Captain John MacDonald of Kirkibost, was a secret Jacobite sympathiser, he, like Armadale, was also a prominent officer in the Hanoverian forces. He therefore had no difficulty in arranging for his wife to make such a journey openly. As Kirkibost was a cousin of Sir Alexander MacDonald, there would be no suspicion attached to his wife making a social visit to Lady Margaret.

She set off for Skye on 27 June. The next day, she arrived at Vaternish, where she was met by a party of soldiers, who subjected her to a strict interrogation and body search.

> 'she was at all the pains imaginable to keep off the soldiers' hands from examining her person too closely'.

Anguier The site chosen as a base for the men trying to find Charles was the uninhabited Priest Island, one of the Summer Isles, four miles from the mouth of Loch Broom. The men hoped they could remain there undetected while they waited for Alexander MacLeod to arrive. The ship anchored off the island late at night on 27 June. After landing some twenty well armed men under the command of Chevalier de Lanzière de Lancize, she set sail for the open sea before midnight.

The Prince
The Prince's companion: Neil MacEachain.

From the summit of Rueval, Charles returned to the booman's bothy, where he was joined by Baleshare. Even though he had not eaten for more than twenty-four hours, Charles was 'very canty and jockose'. He declined Baleshare's offer to exchange his hose for a pair that Charles had accidentally burned, as they were drying by the fire.

Clanranald's bailiff, arrived bearing bread, butter and a roasted hen.

> 'The butter was half salt, as it was what they prepared for cureing their scabed horses; no man cou'd 've tasted it but a starving man.'

However, Charles was so hungry that he ate everything. To quench the effects of eating so much salt, he 'took his bonat and drunk with it out of the loch'.

Later, O'Neil arrived, announcing the imminent arrival of the party from Nunton by

Distant view of the Summer Isles

boat. When they finally arrived, Charles went to welcome them ashore. Charles conducted Lady Clanranald to the bothy, and O'Neil attended to Flora.

While Charles assisted in the roasting of liver, heart and kidneys on a spit, they were all 'very hearty and merry'. At dinner, Flora sat on Charles' right, and Lady Clanranald on his left. No sooner had the meal begun than one of Clanranald's herdsmen arrived to announce that General Campbell was at that moment landing his men just three miles away.

The news caused instant consternation. Immediately, they decided to leave the bothy, and sail to the other side of Loch Uiskevagh, well away from Campbell's troops. In great confusion, they all carried the baggage to the boat. After sailing through the darkness, they landed on the south shore of the loch round about five o'clock in the morning. They found a bothy in which to shelter, and finished the meal that they had abandoned so hastily. They then began the long anxious wait until night, when Charles could sail for Skye under the cover of darkness.

Lady Clanranald wanted to see how well the dress fitted Charles, and 'after mutually passing some jocose drollery', he tried it on. When Charles suggested that he should carry a pistol under the dress, Flora disagreed. She said that if anyone should happen to search Charles, the discovery of a hidden pistol would only give him away. Charles immediately replied with a risqué remark.

'Indeed, Miss,' said Charles, 'if we shall happen to meet with any that will go so narrowly to work in searching as what you mean they will certainly discover me at any rate.'

However, Flora was not in the least put down by this riposte. She stoutly refused to let Charles take any arms at all. Charles' two pistols were therefore left in the safe keeping

'Betty Burke'

of Flora's brother. Charles had to make do with a short heavy cudgel secreted in the folds of his petticoat.

Flora's strength of personality also emerged again when she later refused to take O'Neil to Skye with them. This announcement came as a great shock to Charles, as well as to O'Neil. Both men prevailed on Flora to change her mind. However, Flora reminded Charles that the permit from her stepfather allowed only one man to accompany her, and that this was specified as being MacEachain, in the role of her manservant. She also pointed out that Charles' safety would be greater, the fewer the people making the journey. Having to look after O'Neil, as well as Charles, would simply be adding to her difficulties. In particular, she pointed out that it would be risky to take O'Neil because his 'Foreign air' would make him very conspicuous. Also, his inability to speak Erse would arouse suspicion with anyone they met.

This dispute went on for some time. O'Neil even fell upon his knees imploring Flora to allow him to share Charles' fate, whatever it may be. With great resolution, Flora ignored these pleadings. Eventually O'Neil became resigned to the inevitable. However, Charles announced his refusal to go unless accompanied by O'Neil. In reply, Flora threatened to abort the whole enterprise if Charles continued to insist on taking O'Neil. This remark then prompted an argument between Charles and O'Neil, with O'Neil now threatening to abandon Charles, if Charles would not accept Flora's decision. Eventually, Charles, realising that he had no alternative but to concede, gracefully acknowledged 'the wisdom of her resolution'. In concluding the dispute, it was agreed that O'Neil would follow Charles to Skye when the boat returned in a few days .

Later that morning, a messenger arrived to inform Charles that O'Sullivan had turned up just a few miles away, after making his way from Loch Boisdale. Lady Clanranald went to inform O'Sullivan about Charles' imminent departure for Skye, and arranged for him to stay at her house after Charles left.

Hardly had Lady Clanranald returned to Charles at the loch side, than another a man arrived to give her the fearful news that a party of Campbell's men had arrived at Nunton the previous day. Although Lady Clanranald's youngest daughter had told Fergussone that her mother was away visiting a sick child, he was not satisfied with this excuse. He demanded that she should return immediately. He waited for her arrival, sleeping the night in her bed. In the circumstances, Lady Clanranald had no alternative but to return home before Charles set sail.

The Enemy

At sea, the sloops patrolling the Minch lost contact with the Irish meal ship. Immediately, there was a general alarm, in case Charles had used her to escape. The whole naval force headed south, hoping to find the meal ship off Barra. General Campbell, confident that his sloops would find her there with Charles aboard, immediately rode south from Benbecula.

The Friends

Lady Clanranald On returning to Nunton, Lady Clanranald was interrogated by both Captain Fergussone and General Campbell. The questioning by General Campbell was conducted over dinner.

In order to substantiate her story about visiting a sick child, she had to give the name of the child, and tell them where it lived. Although all her answers were fabricated on the spot, they were so consistent and convincing, that neither Fergussone nor Campbell felt it necessary to check the truth of her story. Satisfied that she had been telling the truth, both men finished their interrogations .

Despite having deceived the enemy, Lady Clanranald realised that she would now be watched very closely. Soon after Fergussone and Campbell left, she sent a message to O'Sullivan telling him that it was not possible now for him to stay with her. However, she did arrange for him to be looked after by some of her clansfolk.

Dumont When *Le Hardi Mendiant* came to anchor in Loch Broom on 28 June, Dumont immediately sent two Irish officers ashore. They managed to convince Rev. Robertson that they had come from the Isle of Man with a cargo of brandy for the ships of the Royal Navy, and that their ship had landed at Loch Broom in order recruit a pilot to take them to Barra. Thus, Rev. Robertson agreed that they could stay in the loch in order to make their arrangements.

The Prince

As the day drew on, the boatmen joined Charles on the south shore of Loch Uiskevagh. There were the two brothers, Rory and John MacDonald, who had scouted up and down South Uist on Charles' behalf. There were also John MacMurrich, Duncan Campbell, and another Rory MacDonald. The boat was a small shallop, of 'about nine cubits, wright measure'. Eventually, O'Neil departed, leaving Charles, Flora and MacEachain to make the final preparations with the crew.

With Flora's assistance, Charles put on the dress. He had trouble adjusting the headdress, which 'he cursed a thousand times'. The whole party then went down to the lochside. When it began to drizzle, the crew made a fire to keep everyone warm. Soon afterwards, a little flotilla of wherries, transporting soldiers, came sailing down the loch towards the sea. Charles and his friends immediately lay in the heather out of sight. However, the wherries turned towards them, attracted by the smoke from the fire. Immediately, the fire was extinguished, and to everyone's great relief, the wherries

changed course back towards the open sea.

At eight o'clock, they set off with John MacDonald at the helm, and four men rowing. The night was now very clear, but, by midnight, rain was falling, and a gale was blowing. Flora was quite distressed by the rough sea. However, Charles was in good heart, and sang Jacobite songs to raise the spirits of his companions. Later, the boat was enveloped in a thick mist. Without a compass, it was impossible to know if they were going in the right direction. John MacDonald therefore decided to heave to, and wait for daylight. Fortunately, the weather became calm, and Flora fell asleep in the bottom of the boat. As the men clambered about the boat, Charles was worried that they might stumble and step on her. When a noise woke her, she found Charles leaning over her with his arms spread out in protection.

By morning, the weather was clear, and the crew found themselves off the west coast of Skye. As they rowed northwards along the coast, the wind changed to blow strongly against them. For an hour and half, they made very little headway. Charles continually encouraged the crew, and offered to take his turn at the oars. Eventually, they landed in a creek on the north corner of Vaternish.

Sound of Orasay, Loch Uiskevagh

85

11
29 JUNE - 1 JULY
SKYE to RAASAY

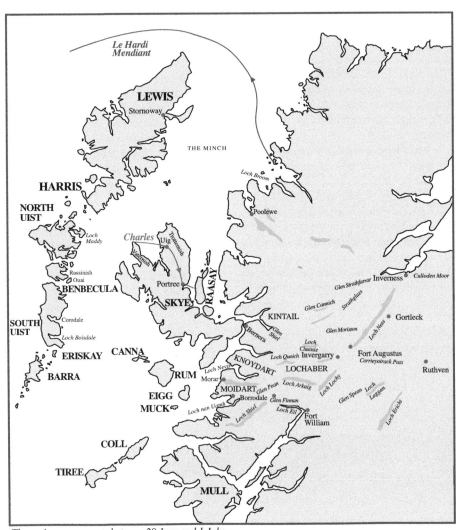

The various movements between 29 June and 1 July

The Friends

O'Neil and O'Sullivan The day after leaving Charles, O'Neil and Flora's brother, Angus, encountered O'Sullivan with Ranald MacEachain. While O'Neil went with Angus to see if his stepfather could arrange accommodation for them, O'Sullivan was taken to an uninhabited island in Loch Uiskevagh. Ranald went to find food, but could not return for thirty hours because the troops were searching the area. During this time, O'Sullivan sheltered from the incessant rain under a rock. He ate shell-fish. Eventually Ranald returned with food. Later, he brought a guide, who took O'Sullivan to another island.

Dumont Although de Lancize and his men were just a few miles away on Priest Island, Dumont was oblivious of their presence. In making his own enquiries about Charles' whereabouts, he soon made contact with Ardloch. Thereby, he learned about the earlier arrival of *Le Lévrier Volant,* and her departure with Captain Lynch to seek Charles in the Outer Isles. Dumont decided to follow the same plan.

With Ardloch's assistance, he press-ganged a pilot from Loch Broom, and set off with Ardloch for the west coast of the Outer Isles. Soon after rounding the Butt of Lewis, he saw a distant ship, which, he knew, would be hostile. As a precautionary measure, Dumont decided to sail to St Kilda, and wait there until the approaches to the Outer Isles were safe.

De Lancize With only a 'wretched hovel' for accommodation, the men on Priest Island were finding life very uncomfortable in the unrelenting cold winds and rain. They were also in continual fear of being discovered, and always had lookouts on duty.

Just four miles to the north-west, *Le Hardi Mendiant* was at anchor off Tanera. Although the lookouts would certainly have noticed her leave, they did not realise that she was a French rescue ship. Thus, no attempt was made to communicate with her. However, Gruinard and his servants did make forays to the mainland to determine whether Alexander MacLeod had arrived. By 1 July, they had received no news of him, so two local men were hired to go further inland to find him.

The Prince

The Prince's companions: Flora MacDonald, Neil MacEachain, Rory MacDonald, John MacDonald, John MacMurrich, Duncan Roy, and Rory MacDonald.

At the creek on Vaternish Point, the exhausted boatmen rested for an hour, and refreshed themselves by drinking from a waterfall. When they set off again, they spotted two sentries on a rock, one of whom shouted an order for the boat to put to. Charles' crew rowed quickly away. After shouting more orders, the sentry cocked his musket, and took aim. However, his musket failed to fire. Meanwhile, his companion had run to a nearby village, and returned with fifteen soldiers.

Vaternish Point

The landing place at Kilbride

Fecklessly, they just walked along the shore, watching Charles' boat disappear into the distance. Had they chosen to board their own boat in pursuit, they would certainly have overtaken Charles and his weary oarsmen.

Charles' crew rowed the twelve miles across Loch Snizort to the Trotternish peninsula, where Lady Margaret MacDonald lived on the west coast at Monkstadt. Just before eleven o'clock in the morning, they landed at Kilbride, a quarter of a mile south of the house.

When MacEachain and Flora approached the house, they were met by a maidservant. She informed them that Sir Alexander was away with Cumberland at Fort Augustus. However, Lady Margaret was at home with Mrs MacDonald from Kirkibost. They were also informed that, at that very moment, Lady Margaret was entertaining two callers. By pure chance, one of them was Alexander MacDonald of Kingsburgh, whom Flora and MacEachain knew to be a Jacobite they could rely upon for help. Much to their horror, the other was Lieutenant Alexander MacLeod, the officer in command of the local detachment of militia. Moreover, he was accompanied by some of his men.

Undeterred, Flora asked to be taken privately to Lady Margaret. On being informed about the new arrivals, while entertaining Lieutenant MacLeod, Lady Margaret became extremely agitated. Somehow, she managed to beckon Kingsburgh inconspicuously away from Lieutenant MacLeod. As the unsuspecting officer waited patiently in the house, Lady Margaret, Kingsburgh, Flora and MacEachain whispered frantically together in the garden. Although Lady Margaret still wanted to hide Charles in her house, Kingsburgh managed to persuade her that, with Lieutenant MacLeod present, it would be too dangerous to bring the Prince there. Kingsburgh also thought Charles should go immediately to a safer resting place, while it was being decided precisely what should be done. He asked MacEachain to take the Prince to the top of a hill about a mile from the house. He also suggested that 'Betty Burke' should be made to look more convincing as a servant. For this purpose, he hurriedly provided MacEachain with some clothes for her to carry.

The ruin of the house at Monkstadt

Lady Margaret MacDonald

MacEachain returned to Charles, and the two of them set off towards the hill, with Charles bearing the awkward bundle. After a short distance, he grew tired, and threw it on the floor. Despite MacEachain's cajoling, Charles refused to pick it up again. He petulantly announced that MacEachain should carry the bundle himself, or leave it where it was. On arriving at the hill, Charles' bad temper continued, and he sat sulking silently for some time. When he spoke, it was to ask if MacEachain had carried a case of knives from the boat. MacEachain answered that he had not. 'Then,' said the prince, 'you must return and look for them.' Astounded, Neil replied, 'Shall I for the sakes of all the knives in the universe leave you here all alone?'

'There will be no fears of me,' said Charles stiffly. 'Do what you are ordered, for I must absolutely have it so no more words.'

MacEachain continued to protest. However, when he realised that Charles was about to fly into a temper, MacEachain reluctantly set off back to the boat, leaving Charles, less than fifty yards from the main road.

Back at the house, Flora, had been interrogated by Lieutenant MacLeod about her journey from Benbecula, but she was soon engaging him in small talk.

Meanwhile, Lady Margaret had sent a message to summon Donald Roy MacDonald. Having been wounded in the foot at Culloden, Donald Roy could not walk very well. He had to make his way to Monkstadt on horseback. On arrival, he found Lady Margaret and Kingsburgh deep in conversation outside the house. As soon as Donald Roy dismounted, Lady Margaret embraced him, and told him the dramatic news of Charles' arrival.

After some hectic discussion, it was agreed that, with the enemy being so close, Charles should leave the area immediately. He should be taken to Raasay, from where he could sail directly to the mainland and comparative safety with the MacKenzies. Initially, Kingsburgh proposed that Charles should sail to Raasay round the top of the Trotternish peninsula. However, Lady Margaret pointed out that, in daylight, Lieutenant MacLeod's lookouts would certainly sound the alarm. Donald Roy then came up with a daring suggestion.

'What would you think, Kingsburgh, if the Prince should run the risque of making his way overland to Portree?'

Desperate though the plan was, Kingsburgh agreed, and offered to take Charles there himself. It was also agreed that Donald Roy would try to secure the help of MacLeod of Raasay, who knew which MacKenzies could be trusted. After arranging to meet Kingsburgh with Charles

that night in Portree, Donald Roy rode off.

Kingsburgh then took his leave of Lady Margaret, and, bearing a bottle of wine and some bread, went to find Charles. However, Charles was not at the place that Kingsburgh had intended. After searching for some time, Kingsburgh began to fear the worst. Suddenly, he saw a flock of sheep bolt. When he went to investigate, he found 'Betty Burke' sitting alone on a rock. As Kingsburgh approached, Charles took out his cudgel, and demanded to know who Kingsburgh was. When Kingsburgh replied, Charles immediately became friendly.

'Then all is well; come let us be jogging on.'

Kinsgburgh explained their latest plan. Fortunately, it suited Charles well, because his own intended destination, Loch Broom, was in MacKenzie country. When MacEachain came back to the boat a few minutes later, Charles was enjoying the bread and wine.

Back at the house, Lady Margaret and Flora were acting out a little charade to deceive Lieutenant MacLeod into thinking that Flora's visit was perfectly normal and above suspicion. In order to avoid conveying any sense of urgency, Flora accepted Lady Margaret's invitation to stay for dinner. However, when Flora was also pressed to stay the night, she declined saying that 'she wanted to see her mother, and to be at home in these troublesome times'.

An hour before sunset, Flora finally left in the company of MacEachain and Kirkibost's wife, who was herself attended by her two servants. While the two ladies rode on horses provided by Lady Margaret, the others walked. Soon, they met Kingsburgh and Charles, waiting on the hill by the road.

Some time before, Kingsburgh had already decided that it was now too late to reach Portree that night. He decided that they should all stay at his house, just eight miles to the south, on the road to Portree. He therefore had sent a message to inform Donald Roy about this change of plan.

Throughout the journey, Charles made a complete travesty of the role of 'Betty Burke'. His strides were far too long for a woman, and he could not handle the dress properly. He also had no idea how to behave as a servant. Instead of attending to her mistress, 'Betty Burke' was brazenly walking ahead, talking confidently with Kingsburgh. The group passed many people walking home from church. 'Betty Burke's' appearance, as well as her behaviour, attracted a great deal of attention. On one occasion, she caused much consternation when, showing no sense of modesty, she raised her skirts too high while crossing a stream.

'For God's sake, Sir,' cried MacEachain, 'Take care what you are doing, for you will certainly discover yourself.'

MacEachain, walking behind, overheard many remarks from people they passed. One man deliberately spoke to MacEachain about her.

'Curse the wretch do you observe, sir what terrible steps she takes, how manly she walks, how carelessly she carries her dress.'

MacEachain claimed to know nothing about the woman, other than that she was an Irish girl, that Flora had met in Uist, and had hired to spin lint.

The situation was made worse by Kirkibost's wife, who kept overtaking Charles in order to see his face. Each time she tried, Charles turned away. It was not long before one of the maids remarked on this behaviour.

She said that

'she had never seen such an impudent-looked woman, and durst say she was either an Irish woman or else a man in a woman's dress'.

Flora assured the maid that 'Betty' was an Irish woman.

Although Charles made light of these incidents, it was now obvious to MacEachain and Flora that 'Betty Burke' was so conspicuous a figure, that it was too dangerous for other people to encounter Charles in this disguise. At the earliest opportunity, Flora and Kirkibost's wife went ahead with the servants. In order not to meet anyone else, Charles and Kingsburgh then completed the rest of journey across open country. Walking through rain, the two men arrived at Kingsburgh's house late at night, just after Flora and the others.

As Kingsburgh's wife was not expecting her husband home that night, she was preparing for bed when he arrived. She was even more surprised when her maid came to her bedroom with news that her husband had brought company with him.

'What company?' said Kingsburgh's wife.

'Milton's daughter, I believe,' said the maid, 'and some company with her.'

'Milton's daughter,' replied Kingsburgh's wife, 'is very welcome to come here with any company she pleases to bring. But you'll give my service to her, and tell her to make free with anything in house; for I am very sleepy and cannot see her this night.'

A few minutes later, Kingsburgh's daughter, Nanie, came rushing to her mother in a state of anxiety.

'O mother, my father has brought in a very odd, muckle, ill-shapen-up wife as ever

I saw! I never saw the like of her, and he has gone into the hall with her.'

At that moment, Kingsburgh himself entered the bedroom. He asked his wife to dress again, and prepare some supper for him and his companions.

'Pray, goodman,' she said, 'what company is this you brought with you?'

'Why, goodwife', he said, 'you shall know that in due time; only make haste and get some supper in the meantime.'

Kingsburgh's wife then asked Nanie to fetch her keys from the hall. Almost immediately, the girl came running back, saying that she could not go in for the keys, because she was frightened by the strange woman. When Kingsburgh's wife went to investigate, she saw 'an odd muckle trallup of a carlin, making lang wide steps through the hall'. She then called her husband and demanded to know 'what a lang, odd hussie was this he had brought to the house'.

'Did you never see a woman before, goodwife. What frights you at seeing a woman? Pray, make haste, and get us some supper.'

When Kingsburgh's wife finally got her keys, and entered the hall, Charles was sitting. Immediately, he rose and kissed her hand. The lady felt his long stiff beard, and realised that the strange character was a man in disguise. Without saying a word, she left the room. As soon as she had the opportunity to talk to her husband privately, she asked who the man was.

'Why, my dear, it is the Prince. You have the honour to have him in your house.'

'The Prince!' she cried, 'O Lord, we are a' ruin'd and undone for ever! We will a' be hang'd now!'

'Hout, goodwife,' replied Kingsburgh, 'we will die but once; and if we are hanged for this, I am sure we die in a good cause.

Pray, make no delay; go, get some supper. Fetch what is readiest. You have eggs and butter and cheese in the house, get them as quickly as possible.'

'Eggs and butter and cheese!' exclaimed his wife, 'what a supper is that for a Prince?'

'O goodwife, little do you know how this good Prince has been living for some time past. These, I can assure you, will be a feast to him. Besides, it would be unwise to be dressing a formal supper, because this would serve to raise the curiosity of the servants, and they would be making their observations. The less ceremony and work the better. Make haste, and see that you come to supper.'

'I come to supper,' she cried, 'how can I come to supper? I know not how to behave before Majesty.'

'You must come,' said Kingsburgh, 'for he will not eat a bit till he see you at the table; and you will find it no difficult matter to behave before him, so obliging and easy is he in his conversation.'

Charles' supper was roasted eggs and collops with plenty of bread and butter. In addition, 'the deel a drap did he want in's weam of twa bottles of sma beer.' Afterwards, he called for a dram, and on being presented with a bottle of brandy, he said he would fill the glass himself, 'for,' said he, 'I have learn'd in my skulking to take a hearty dram.' Next, he took one of the cracked broken pipes from his pouch, and asked Kingsburgh if there was any tobacco in the house. Kingsburgh would not allow Charles to use this pipe. Laying it carefully to one side, he provided a new pipe together with plenty of tobacco.

Late though it was, the conversation continued for some time. With the aid of more brandy, Charles and Kingsburgh became good friends. As Kingsburgh had been at Monkstadt that morning purely by chance, he asked what Charles would have done if they had not met there.

'Why, sir,' replied Charles, 'you could not avoid being at Mougstot this day; for Providence ordered you to be there upon my account.'

That night, Charles slept in a proper bed for the first time in nearly twelve weeks. He continued to sleep soundly long after everybody else had woken up. As Flora was anxious not to delay their departure, she asked Kingsburgh to wake Charles. Initially, he refused because he knew that Charles may not have an opportunity for sleeping comfortably again for some time. Only after much persuasion by Flora, did he reluctantly go up to Charles' bedroom. However, when he saw Charles sleeping so deeply, Kingsburgh came out of the room without waking him.

As Flora waited impatiently for Charles to wake, she told Kinsburgh's wife of her adventures with Charles. Kingsburgh's wife eventually plucked up courage to say that she wanted a lock of Charles' hair, and asked Flora to go to Charles' room to cut one for her. Flora refused, because Charles was not yet awake. However, her hostess persisted.

'What then,' she said, 'no harm will come to you. He is too good to harm you or any person. You must instantly go in and get me the lock.'

Determined to get her way, Kingsburgh's wife led Flora upstairs and knocked on Charles' door. When Charles answered, Kingsburgh's wife opened the door.

'Sir, it is I, and I am importuneing Miss Flora to come and get a lock of your hair to me, and she refuses to do it.'

'Pray,' said the Prince, 'desire Miss MacDonald to come in. What should make her afraid to come where I am?'

Charles then asked Flora to sit on a chair by the bed. Laying his arms about her waist, and his head upon her lap, he asked her to cut the lock. Whereupon, Flora gave half the lock to her hostess, and kept the remainder for herself.

At this point, Kingsburgh arrived, and asked Charles how he had rested.

'Never better,' he replied, 'for I have rested exceedingly well, having slept, I believe, nine or ten hours without interruption.'

Kingsburgh then suggested that Charles should not continue to dress as 'Betty Burke', because he was 'very bad at acting the part of a dissembler'. Instead, Kingsburgh offered to give Charles a suit of Highland clothes and a broadsword, which 'would become him much better'. However, he advised Charles to leave the house as 'Betty Burke', and change into the new clothes soon afterwards. In this way, Kingsburgh hoped that the servants would not realise that 'Betty Burke' was a man in disguise. Also, if they did, they would not know the sort of clothes he changed into.

Kingsburgh's wife entrusted Nanie with the responsibility of dressing Charles in his woman's clothes.

'For the deel a preen he could put in.'

In the process, there was much hilarity. Kingsburgh and his wife were amazed that, despite the danger of his predicament, Charles was as carefree as if he were dressing in women's clothes 'merely as a diversion'. Flora put the finishing touches to his cap.

It was late in the day when they were ready to depart for Portree. Just as they were leaving the house, Charles turned and said, 'Can none of you give me a snuff?' Immediately, Kingsburgh's wife offered some from a silver mill, which Kingsburgh begged Charles to keep. Accordingly, Charles put the mill into the pouch hanging by his side. Kingsburgh then led Charles, Flora and MacEachain to a wood not far from the house.

There, they stopped so that Charles could change into a plaid. After presenting Flora with 'Betty Burke's' garters, which were 'French of blue velvet covered upon one side with white silk, and fastened with buckles', the rest of the dress was hidden in a thicket.

Kingsburgh now took his leave. Tearfully, the two men embraced each other, with Charles thanking Kingsburgh, and assuring him he would never be forgotten. In the process, Charles suffered a sudden nose-bleed, which so alarmed Kingsburgh that he wanted to take Charles back to the house. Charles made light of it, and found a remedy in cold water. 'This,' said he, ' is only the effect of parting with a dear friend, and ordinarily it happens in such a case. Alas! Kingsburgh, I am afraid I shall not meet with another MacDonald in my difficulties.' He was relieved, when Kingsburgh assured him that Donald Roy would accompany him to Raasay.

Charles then set off. In a pocket of his plaid, he carried four shirts, a cold chicken, a bottle of brandy and a lump of sugar. While Flora rode alone on the main road, Charles and MacEachain walked on the open ground at some distance from the road. They were guided by a young boy recruited by Kingsburgh. It began to rain heavily soon after they left. During the seven-mile journey, they were soaked. By the time they arrived at Portree, it was dark.

They had planned to meet Donald Roy at an inn. While they were some distance away, Charles and MacEachain sent the boy ahead to ask Donald Roy to come out and speak with them. Donald Roy limped out into the rain to meet them. Charles immediately embraced Donald Roy, and warned him against performing any act of obeisance in case they were observed by some enemy.

As soon as Charles walked into the inn, he called for a dram, which he drank before sitting down. He then ordered food. Because Flora was in the room, he resisted the urgings of his friends to change his soaking clothes. However, when both Donald Roy and MacEachain insisted that this was not the time for decorum, Charles changed his shirt. Wearing nothing else, he sat, eating roasted fish and cheese with bread and butter. As he ate, Charles looked up, and noticed Donald Roy smiling.

Sir, I believe that is the English fashion,' said Donald Roy.

'What fashion do you mean?' asked Charles.

'Why,' replied Donald Roy, 'they say the English, when they are to eat heartily throw off their cloaths.'

Smiling, Charles replied, 'They are in the right, lest anything should incommode their hands when they are at work.'

The only drink available was water. It had to be drunk directly from an old bucket used by the landlord for bailing his boat. Charles was aghast when he saw how broken and unsavoury it looked. However, Donald Roy, whispered to Charles that he must drink from it without complaint. Otherwise, the landlord, who was looking on, would be suspicious.

'You are right,' said Charles, and took a hearty draught.

Later, Charles bought tobacco and a bottle of whisky, which he shared with Donald Roy and MacEachain. Donald Roy now informed Charles that he had some friends waiting nearby with a boat to take him to Raasay. Pointing to the rain, still falling heavily, Charles wanted to delay the journey, and suggested that they stay the night where they were. However, Donald Roy persuaded him against this plan, because the inn was frequented by people who would be curious about a stranger.

As Donald Roy described the plans for the journey, Charles realised that, despite Kingsburgh's assurances, Donald Roy did not intend to accompany him. Donald Roy explained that his wounded foot would be a handicap to everyone. He had therefore arranged for Charles to make the journey with the MacLeods.

This proposal alarmed Charles, as it meant leaving the MacDonalds, on whom he had grown to depend totally. He said he would not feel safe unless a MacDonald were with him, and begged Donald Roy to come with him. Donald Roy agreed to come only if Charles were to stay in one place. If he were to move from place to place, the wounded foot would be too painful. However, Donald Roy insisted on remaining alone on Skye for a few days in order to find out whether the enemy had discovered where Charles had gone. He promised to join Charles on Raasay later.

Charles was still not satisfied. 'Are you afraid to go along with me?' he asked. 'I can assure you so long as I have you I shall not want. I still am anxious to have a MacDonald along with me.'

Again, Donald Roy rehearsed his argument about the wounded foot. Eventually, Charles reluctantly had to accept the situation.

As they were about to leave the inn, Charles decided that he did not have enough small coins, and asked Donald Roy to change a golden guinea for twenty-one silver coins with the landlord. When Donald Roy reported that the landlord had only eleven silver coins, Charles said that he would willingly accept them for the guinea. However, Donald Roy refused to strike the bargain, saying that such rash generosity would only arouse the landlord's suspicions. Donald Roy also took this incident as an opportunity to enquire how the Prince stood financially, and indicated that 'he knew a friend in that country ready and willing to supply him'. When Charles enquired who this potential benefactor might be, Donald Roy revealed that it was Lady Margaret MacDonald. Charles said that, although he was obliged to Lady Margaret for her concern, he had sufficient money for his immediate purposes.

As it was now nearly dawn, Donald Roy was anxious to get to the boat. Despite Donald Roy's continual urgings, Charles lingered for some minutes to take his leave of Flora and MacEachain.

'I believe, Madam, I owe you a crown of borrowed money.'

Flora told him it was actually only half-a-crown. He then kissed her hand, and said, 'For all that has happened I hope Madam, we shall meet in St James's yet.'

Then, after tying a bottle of whisky to one side of his belt, and a bottle of brandy, together with the shirts and the cold chicken to the other, he made for the door.

As they left, Donald Roy noticed the landlord looking after them. Donald Roy therefore deliberately started to lead Charles in a direction away from the boat. Only when they were out of the landlord's sight, did he turn along the right path.

The boat was no more than half a mile from the inn. Young Raasay was waiting by it with his brother, Dr Murdoch MacLeod, and their cousin, Malcolm MacLeod. There were also two boatmen, John MacKenzie and Donald MacFriar. As soon as Charles clambered aboard, Donald Roy introduced him to the MacLeods. Charles insisted that they should not bow or kneel.

Again, Charles tried to persuade Donald Roy to come with him, but, after a brief consultation with the MacLeods, Donald Roy confirmed his original plan. However, it was agreed that Young Raasay would come to collect Donald Roy from Skye in three days' time.

Before leaving, Charles' thoughts turned to Flora, because he knew she would now be in great danger if the troops discovered her part in his escape from Benbecula. He took the lump of sugar from his pocket, and, giving it to Donald Roy, said, 'Pray, MacDonald, take this piece of sugar to our lady, for I am afraid she will get no sugar where she is going.' There then followed an extended exchange in which Donald Roy refused to accept the gift, and Charles kept insisting that he did. In the end, Donald Roy, accepted the sugar, but surreptitiously slipped it into Malcolm MacLeod's hand, whispering that it should be kept for Charles' use. Charles' last request to Donald Roy also concerned Flora's safety.

'Tell nobody, no not our lady, which way I am gone, for it is right that my course should not be known.'

During the voyage, Charles thanked the MacLeods for their help, saying that 'friends who show'd their friendship in distress were the reall friends, and that he hoped his friends would not have reason to repent for the services done him'. After about half an hour, they landed on the west coast of Raasay, near the settlement of Glam.

Portree harbour

12
1 - 4 JULY
RAASAY to SKYE

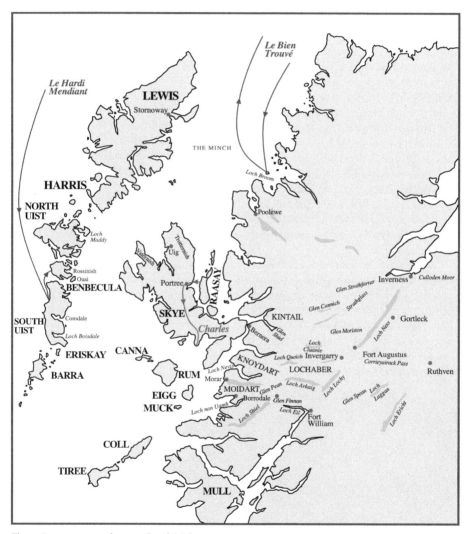

The various movements between 1 and 4 July

The Friends

O'Neil and O'Sullivan When the boatmen who had taken Charles to Skye, returned to Benbecula, they brought a note from Charles, asking O'Neil to follow him to Skye. However, the boatmen, having been frightened by the incident with the troops at Vaternish, refused to make the journey a second time. O'Neil was therefore unable to leave for Skye. Instead, he was taken to join O'Sullivan on the island in Loch Uiskevagh. After one night there, they were taken to the house of MacDonald of Torlum, where they 'found good Straw & thought themselfs happy'.

Dumont After the brief soujourn off St Kilda, Dumont sailed *Le Hardi Mendiant* back to the Outer Isles. On 3 July, he anchored off South Uist in the Howmore estuary. Here, he learned from the locals that O'Neil and O'Sullivan were on Benbecula. He turned north to find them, and arrived off Benbecula very early the next day.

De Lancize In their misery on Priest Island, de Lancize and his men had run out of food. They were also were beginning to be sick. It was to their great relief that *Le Bien Trouvé* arrived on 3 July. Having despaired of meeting Alexander MacLeod, the Frenchmen were on the verge of sailing south to Lochaber, when he arrived.

He advised them that it would be impossible for them to find Charles now, and advised them to leave for France that very day. However, the Frenchmen refused to give up the search. Knowing that Lochiel and Murray of Broughton had written to Charles asking him to return to the mainland, MacLeod suggested that they should look for Charles at Loch Arkaig. Anguier decided to send two men there on independent missions. Accordingly, de Lancize, and a Franco-Irishman, de Belieu, were put ashore, dressed 'in the garb of the country'. MacLeod also told Anguier that it would be unsafe for the ship to remain in Loch Broom, because Rev. Robertson had already informed Cumberland of the ship's presence. Anguier therefore set sail, intending to cruise off the Orkneys before returning to Loch Broom in about five weeks.

The Prince

The Prince's companions: John MacLeod (Raasay's son), Dr Murdoch MacLeod, Captain Malcolm MacLeod, John MacKenzie and Donald MacFriar.

As all the houses on Raasay had been destroyed during Fergussone's rampage, the only accommodation that could be offered to Charles was a miserable

Inbhir near Glam, Raasay

ramshackle hut. It was so low that Charles 'could neither sitt nor stand, but was obliged to lie on the bare ground'. Charles now learned that Old Raasay was currently hiding on the mainland in Knoydart, and that a message had been sent to summon him. They lit a fire, and ate the food brought from Kingsburgh. Much to the approval of the MacLeods, Charles announced his preference for bread made from oats rather than wheat, and for whisky rather than brandy.

'For these are my own country's bread and drink.'

He then rested, while Young Raasay, the only one of the party who could walk about openly on the island, went in search of more food. He returned after two hours with a young kid, fresh cream, and butter.

With several days to wait before Donald Roy and Old Raasay could join them, Charles wanted to find out if a French rescue ship had arrived at Loch Broom. Young Raasay therefore sent a letter asking for news to the mainland at Applecross, just eight miles across the water.

Meanwhile, the MacLeods took Charles for a short walk to see the devastation the island had suffered. Deeply affected, Charles promised his friends that the wooden huts, which Fergussone's men had burned down, would be replaced with houses of stone. Charles was also very concerned that Murdoch's shoulder wound, from Culloden, was still causing pain.

When the conversation turned to his own deprivations, he acknowledged that life had been a little hard in recent times. However, he said that he would rather live ten years in that way than be taken by his enemies. He was surprised how well he had been able to stand up to the conditions, and ascribed his resilience to divine help.

'Since the battle of Culloden, I have endured more than would kill a hundred. Some Providence does not design this for nothing.'

While Young Raasay spent the night in his own house, Charles slept with Murdoch and Malcolm in the hut, guarded by John MacKenzie and Donald MacFriar. His sleep was fitful. In a nightmare brought on by the terrible sights he had seen that day, his anguished cries woke the others up.

'O God! Poor Scotland!'

The next day, a letter came from Applecross saying that there had been 'no appearance of any French ship' at Loch Broom. As Loch Broom is some fifty miles to the north, it is not surprising that the residents of Applecross were unaware of the arrival of *Le Hardi Mendiant* and *Le Bien Trouvé* . However, it is ironic that, on the very day that Charles received this misleading information, *Le Bien Trouvé* had just returned to Loch Broom.

Despite the assurances of the MacLeods that he was perfectly safe, Charles felt that the island of Raasay was too confined to ensure his safety. However, acting on the incorrect information from Applecross, Charles decided not to risk the dangers of the sixty-mile sea journey direct to Loch Broom. With the aim of making his way to Loch Broom via Skye, he insisted on sailing to Portree that night.

As they whiled away the rest of the day, the lookouts reported a man walking towards the hut. On closer inspection, he was recognised as a tobacco salesman, who had arrived on the island two weeks previously. Having sold his stock, he had mysteriously stayed on. The residents of Raasay suspected that he was a government spy.

The closer he approached, the more

worried the MacLeods became. They decided that, if he came to the hut, he must be shot, because he would inevitably catch sight of Charles. Charles immediately protested.

'God forbid that we should take any poor man's life, while we can save our own.'

As the argument continued, the man passed by, oblivious of Charles' presence, and of his own close approach to death.

In the evening, the boat was launched in heavy rain and a strong wind. Charles set off for Skye, accompanied by the three MacLeods and the two boatmen. Very soon, the gale became so bad, that the waves were coming over the boat. Malcolm MacLeod had to start bailing out the water. When Charles' companions decided that they should return to Raasay, he refused to do so. He tried to raise their spirits by singing a song in Erse, and shouted, 'Gentlemen, I hope to thank you for this trouble yet at St James.'

Fortunately, they landed safely on Nicholson's Rock, with Charles as relieved as any of them.

'God be thanked we are safe here.'

Charles jumped out of the boat calling, 'Take care of the boat, and hawl her up to the dry ground.' He then set to this task with the others. By now, they were all soaked. Charles' topcoat was so heavy and cumbersome that Malcolm MacLeod wanted to carry it up the steep rocks from the shore. However, Charles declined the offer, saying that he was able to carry it just as well as Malcolm.

The only accommodation, that they knew to be nearby, was a cow byre, which Young Raasay went to reconnoitre. Charles' companions were worried that, he would perish before daylight. They asked him what he would do if the cow byre were occupied.

'I don't care a button for it,' he replied, 'for I have been without a hundred such nights.'

Fortunately, Young Raasay brought back the good news that the byre was free. They all therefore made their way there.

Having lit a fire, and eaten some bread and cheese, they made plans for the morning. Young Raasay was detailed to find Donald Roy, and bring him to the byre the next day. As they talked, Charles obstinately refused Malcolm's suggestion to put on a dry shirt, and take some sleep. However, tiredness soon overcame him. He fell asleep by the fire in his wet clothes.

Next morning, Young Raasay rose early, and set off on his mission. While Malcolm and the two boatmen mounted guard outside, Charles, attended by Murdoch, slept soundly in the byre until mid-day. On waking, he insisted that Malcolm and the boatmen should now sleep, while he and Murdoch took their turn at guard duty. As evening came, Charles became impatient for Young Raasay and Donald Roy to arrive. Eventually, he announced that he would wait only until eight o'clock. Then, he would leave, even if they had not appeared. He asked Murdoch if he could walk well. When Murdoch said his wound still hampered him, Charles asked Murdoch whether Malcolm could walk well, and be trusted. Murdoch assured Charles that he could trust Malcolm with his life. Whereupon, Charles revealed his plan to Murdoch.

Charles intended to travel overnight with Malcolm to the other side of Skye, where he hoped to find a boat that would take him to the island of Rum. If he failed, they would return, and try to sail from the east cost of Skye. In that case, he would meet Murdoch, Young Raasay and Donald Roy in three days' time at Camastianavaig, about three miles south of Portree. In the meantime, Murdoch was to prepare his other boat to take Charles to the mainland. If that journey was considered too risky, Donald Roy was to make alternative arrangements for Charles to sail to the mainland from Sleat. After emphasising how important it was for Murdoch 'to take particular care to manage aright, as it is an affair of great consequence', Charles and Murdoch went into the byre to acquaint Malcolm with the plan.

Charles began by asking Malcolm if he was a stout walker, and if he could walk barefoot. When Malcolm assured Charles on both counts, Charles explained that by 'barefoot', he meant being able to walk in shoes but without stockings. Somewhat puzzled by these questions, Malcolm said he had never tried to do that, and therefore did not know. He then interrupted this interrogation by announcing that he could see a man coming down the hillside above the byre. Immediately, Murdoch urged Charles and Malcolm to leave. Hastily gathering his bundle and cudgel together, Charles asked Murdoch to look after a silver spoon, knife and fork for him. He also tore out the buckles from his shoes, and wrapped himself in his plaid in order to look like an ordinary man. As they left the byre, Malcolm took hold of Charles' bundle, saying, 'Give me that.'

Silently, they walked until they were out of sight of the byre. Charles then took a turning that alarmed Malcolm.

'Your royal highness will pardon me to ask where you are going, for that I dread you may chance to fall into the hands of some party or another, if you do not take exceeding good care, as there are many small parties dispersed up and down the country.'

Charles now revealed his plan to Malcolm.

'Why, MacLeod, I now throw myself entirely into your hands, and leave you to do with me what you please. Only I want to go to Strath, MacKinnon's country. I hope you will accompany me, and you think you can lead me safe enough into Strath.'

Malcolm assured Charles that he would go anywhere Charles pleased, and that he could certainly do so safely, provided they went by sea. He also said that a journey by land would be dangerous, because there were so many troops in the area. However, Charles insisted on going by land, saying that he could not do anything now without running risks. In the ensuing argument, Charles tried to undermine Malcolm's protests by claiming that he knew the way there very well himself.

Unconvinced, Malcolm replied, 'I am sure I must know it much better, and I must tell you that we have a long journey to make, no less that 24 or 30 long miles. For I dare not lead you the direct road, but take you byways, and go here and there cross the country to keep free as we can of the parties scattered up and down.'

Charles also brushed aside Malcolm's suggestion that they wait until morning. He insisted on leaving immediately, and travelling overnight. Although he was daunted by the responsibility and danger ahead, Malcolm had to agree.

Charles proposed to pass himself off as Malcolm's servant, 'Lewie Caw'. Charles would carry all the luggage, and walk a respectful distance behind Malcolm. During the journey, Malcolm expected to meet friends or acquaintances, whom he would have to engage in polite

conversation. Otherwise, he might cause offence, or
create suspicion. He told Charles to show no concern
when such encounters occurred. Charles was just to
wait, as a servant would do, sitting at some distance
from his master.

The Cuillins from Sligachan

The journey took them over high ridges, across
wild moors, and through the remote Strath Mor.
Despite the difficulty of the terrain, they walked
quickly in order to pass the army camp at Glen
Sligachan during the night. In the dark, Charles fell
into a bog almost to the top of his thighs. Malcolm had
to pull him out by the armpits. When dawn broke,
Charles was astounded at the sight of the high hills
surrounding him.

'I am sure the Devil cannot find us now.'

Charles perspired heavily, stopping frequently to drink
water. Malcolm advised him to take a dram with the
water, and warned that it was not healthy to drink water
while sweating. Charles disagreed.

'No, no. That will never hurt me in the least.
If you happen to drink any cold thing when you are
warm, only remember, MacLeod, to piss after drinking,
and it will do you no harm at all. This advice I had
from a friend abroad.'

On reaching the last dram of brandy, each man insisted

that the other should have it. After a long argument, Malcolm again conceded, and emptied the bottle, which Charles then wanted to break and throw away.

'No, no,' said Malcolm, 'I will be far from breaking it that I will do my best to preserve it as a curious piece. It may come to drink many a cask of whiskie to me yet.'

He then hid the bottle in a bush, intending to retrieve it later. He hoped that 'the bottle would make a figure in Westminster yet'.

In another rest, while taking snuff from the mill that Kingsburgh's wife had given him, Charles asked Malcolm, the meaning of the motto 'ROB GIB' that was carved on it.

'Why,' said Malcolm, 'that is the emblem we use in Scotland to represent a

Glamaig and Beinn Dearg Mhor from Sligachan

Marsco and Mam a' Phobuill from Sligachan

103

firm and strong friendship, and the common saying is Rob Gib's contract, stark love and kindness.'

'Well, MacLeod, ' said Charles, 'for that very same cause shall I endeavour to keep the mill all my life.'

Malcolm noticed that Charles was continually scratching his body. On unbuttoning Charles' shirt, he saw that Charles was infested with lice. Malcolm then removed 'four score' of them.

During their journey, Charles spoke of his

Strath Mor

hopes for the future.

'MacLeod, do you not think that God Almighty has made this person of mine for doing some good yet? When I was in Italy, and dining at the king's table, very often the sweat would have been coming through my coat with the heat of the climate; and now that I am in a cold country, of a more piercing and trying climate, and exposed to different kinds of fatigues, I really find I agree equally with both. I have had this philibeg on now for some days, and I find I do as well with it as any the best breeches I ever put on. I hope in God, MacLeod, to walk the streets of London with it yet.'

Charles then remarked that his scarlet

tartan waistcoat with gold twist buttons, was altogether too grand for a servant. He therefore exchanged it for Malcolm's.

'I hope, MacLeod, to give you a much better vest for this yet.'

As there had been many MacKinnons in Charles' army, Malcolm was worried that Charles would be recognised in MacKinnon country. On approaching their destination, Malcolm suggested that Charles should disguise himself more effectively. Charles took off his periwig, and asked Malcolm to tie a dirty white napkin round his head so that it came down over his eyes and nose. He then pulled his bonnet over the napkin.

'I think I will now pass well enough for your servant, and that I am sick with much fatigue I have undergone. Look at me, MacLeod, and tell me what you think. How will it do?'

When Malcolm said that he thought Charles would still be recognised, Charles was a little put out.

'This is an odd remarkable face I have got that nothing can disguise it.'

Malcolm's view was confirmed shortly afterwards, when Charles was recognised by two MacKinnons. Lifting their hands in despair, they 'wept bitterly to see him such a pickle'. Malcolm immediately urged them to stop their histrionics in case they drew the attention of other travellers to Charles. Then, he made them swear not to tell anyone that they had seen the Prince in that part of the country.

Malcolm's sister lived at Elgol with

her husband, John MacKinnon, a captain in Charles' army. Malcolm decided to go to their house first. They arrived during the morning. Leaving Charles at some distance from the house, Malcolm went to find out if it was safe for them to stay. When his sister assured him that there were no troops in the area, Malcolm introduced 'Lewie Caw' to her. On entering the house, 'Lewie' took off his bonnet, made a low bow to Malcolm's sister, and sat at some distance from his master. While Malcolm's sister prepared a meal, she remarked that 'there was something about that lad that she liked unco well, and she could not help admiring his looks'.

The Cuillins from Elgol

When bread, cheese and milk were served, Malcolm invited 'Lewie' to share it. However, 'Lewie' declined, saying that 'he knew better manners'. Only when Malcolm ordered him to do so did 'Lewie' start to eat it.

Afterwards, Malcolm asked a maidservant to wash his feet and legs, as they were covered in mud from the journey. As she did so, he said, 'You see that poor sick man there, I hope you'll wash his feet too. It will be a great charity, for he has as much need as I have.'

Very much affronted, the woman protested.

'No such thing! Although I wash the master's feet, I am not obliged to wash the servant's. What! He's but a low countrywoman's son. I will not wash his feet indeed.'

Eventually, Malcolm was able to persuade the woman to change her mind. As she washed him,

Charles nearly gave himself away by complaining about her rough touch.

'O MacLeod, if you would desire the girl not to go so far up.'

Malcolm now urged Charles to sleep, and offered to keep guard himself. Immediately, Charles threw himself, fully dressed on a bed. Malcolm then asked his puzzled sister to keep watch from a knoll outside the house, so that he could sleep as well.

When Malcolm's sister woke him with news that her husband was coming, Malcolm went out to meet him. After greeting his brother-in-law, Malcolm pointed to the ships cruising off shore.

'What if our Prince be on board one of them?'

'God forbid!' replied John, 'I would not wish that for anything.'

'What,' said Malcolm, 'if we had him here, John? Do you think he would in safety enough?'

'I wish with all my heart we had him here,' replied John, 'for he would be safe enough'.

'Well then,' said Malcolm, 'he is here already. He is just now in your house. But when you go in you must be careful to take no notice of him at all. He passes for 'Lewie Caw', my servant.'

Nervously, John entered his house intending to dissemble, as instructed by Malcolm. However, he could not stop himself from staring at Charles, who was carrying the MacKinnons' young son, Neil, and singing. When Charles looked up and said, 'I hope this child may be a captain in my service yet.' John was overcome with emotion. All he could do was turn away, his eyes full of tears.

Charles' new host was a man of passionate and heroic loyalty. For him, it was the greatest of honours to harbour the Prince in his humble home, and he was delighted to offer his help in transporting Charles to the mainland.

Both Malcolm and Charles were reluctant to involve the Laird of MacKinnon. Although he was a man of great spirit, courage and unquestioning loyalty to the Jacobite cause, Old MacKinnon was somewhat senile and infirm. It was therefore agreed that John would operate alone in hiring a boat on behalf of Malcolm. However, when John left to carry out this mission, and accidentally met Old MacKinnon on the way, he could not stop himself from telling his chief the news.

Immediately, the old man insisted on taking charge, and undertook to find a boat. When John went back to report to the others, Malcolm wanted to return home, and leave Charles in the good hands of Old MacKinnon. Once again, Charles did not want to part from a friend on whom he had depended for so much. He therefore would not agree to Malcolm's leaving. However, Malcolm insisted. He knew that his absence may well have been noted back in Raasay, and that it would be dangerous for him to stay away any longer. Indeed, he expected to be arrested when he returned.

'And no matter for that at all,' he said, 'if it can tend to promote your safety, which it cannot readily fail to do.' Reluctantly, Charles had to agree.

Unlike most chiefs, Old MacKinnon had led his clansmen personally in the invasion of England. True to character, he now insisted on accompanying Charles to the mainland. As promised, Old MacKinnon had procured a small rowing boat, and arranged their departure for the late evening. He assembled a crew comprising John MacRory, Vic Lauchlan, Calum MacGuinness and John MacGuinness.

As the crew made the final preparations, Old MacKinnon and his wife ate a meal with Charles in a cave by the shore at Port a Luig Mhoir. Malcolm MacLeod came to see them off. When some enemy ships appeared off shore, Malcolm urged Charles to wait to see in which direction the ships sailed, before setting off.

'For just now, the wind blows so as to fetch them this way and to hinder you passing to the continent.'

The Prince replied, 'Never fear, MacLeod, I'll go on board directly. The wind will change immediately and make these ships steer a contrary course. Providence will take care of me, and it will not be in the power of these ships to look near at this time.'

Before climbing into the boat, Charles turned to Malcolm and said, 'Don't you remember that I promised to meet Murdoch MacLeod at such a place?'

'No matter,' said Malcolm. 'I shall make your apology.'

'That's not enough,' said Charles, 'Have you paper, pen and ink upon you MacLeod?' I'll write him a few lines. I'm obliged so to do in good manners.'

In order not incriminate its recipient, the letter contained an innocent-looking message, and was signed with a *nom de plume*.

'I thank God I am in good health, and have got off as design'd. Remember me to all friends, and thank them for the trouble they have been at.

I am, Sir,
Your humble servant,
JAMES THOMSON'

(4 July, 1746)   *Port a Luig Mhoir*

As he handed over the letter, Charles asked Malcolm to light his pipe. Obligingly, Malcolm kindled some tow by holding it near the powder pan of a gun, which he fired. He then held the tow near the mouth of a 'cutty,' in Charles' mouth. Unfortunately the 'cutty' was very short, and Charles' cheek was scorched.

Despite this minor accident, Charles presented Malcolm with a silver stock-buckle. In a final parting embrace, he pressed ten guineas into Malcolm's hand. Malcolm stoutly refused to accept the money, saying that Charles would have a greater need for it. However, Charles insisted, saying that he wished it had been much more. After expressing a final regret that Malcolm was not accompanying him to the mainland, he ordered the boatmen to set off.

Malcolm sat on the shore watching the boat disappear. After a short while, he was amazed to find that, as Charles predicted, the wind changed, blowing the enemy ships out of sight.

'Mr MacLeod affirm'd that in all the course of his life he had never known any man that had such a firm trust and well-grounded confidence as the Prince was remarkably endued with.'

The cave at Port a Luig Mhoir

13
4 - 8 JULY
SKYE to MORAR

The various movements between 4 and 8 July

The Enemy

As Campbell's men continued their relentless search on South Uist, they apprehended Donald MacLeod on 5 July. Having lost touch with Charles over a fortnight previously, any information Donald could give was obviously out-of-date. Knowing that Charles had already escaped from Benbecula, Donald told the troops what he knew, for what it was worth. He was treated relatively leniently in his interrogation.

The Friends

O'Neil, O'Sullivan and Dumont As soon as *Le Hardi Mendiant* anchored off the west coast of Benbecula, a party was sent ashore. In the early hours of the morning, it was conducted to Torlum's house, where O'Neil and O'Sullivan were lodged. Immediately, O'Neil and O'Sullivan went aboard the cutter, and reported that Charles had left Benbecula only a few days before.

It was then agreed that O'Neil would try to bring Charles back. For this purpose, Torlum offered to find him a boat and crew. In the meantime, the cutter would sail into the safety of the open sea, and return after four days. Although O'Sullivan wanted to wait for O'Neil on Benbecula, Torlum insisted that O'Sullivan should also go off in the cutter, because his presence on Benbecula would be a danger to them all. They therefore all went their separate ways.

In a very confused account , written a year afterwards, O'Neil claimed to have made his way to Raasay in his search for Charles. However, bearing in mind that O'Neil did not know that Charles was in Raasay, and that O'Neil was arrested by the troops in Benbecula on 6 July, it seems that these claims are as erroneous and exaggerated as many of the others that he made subsequently. It is more likely that O'Neil never set off on this mission, and that he remained on Benbecula.

After his arrest, O'Neil was taken on board the *Furnace*, and interrogated by Fergussone.

' [Captain Ferguson] used me with all the barbarity of a pirate, stripped me, and had ordered me to be put into a rack and whipped by his hangman, because I would not confess where I thought the Prince was. As I was just going to be whipped, being already stripped, Lieutenant MacCaghan of the Scotch Fusileers, who commanded a party under Captain Ferguson, very generously opposed this barbarous usage, and coming out with his drawn sword threatened Captain Ferguson that he'd sacrifice himself and his detachment rather that to see an officer used after such an infamous manner.'

From this interrogation, Fergussone learned the whole story of how Charles, dressed as a maidservant had escaped to Skye with Flora MacDonald. On learning that Armadale, as well as Lady Clanranald, had been involved in the plot, orders were given for their arrests. O'Neil also divulged that Charles was intending to seek the help of the MacKinnons on Skye.

De Lancize and De Belieu After the departure of *Le Bien Trouvé*, de Lancize and de Belieu realised that their chances of surviving were very slim. They were alone in a strange land, unable to speak the language, and unable to find their way around. After one more stormy night on Priest Island, their morale was so low that they decided not to set out on their mission. Instead, they made their way to a neighbouring island, where they intended to stay until *Le Bien Trouvé* returned.

The Prince

The Prince's companions: Old MacKinnon, John MacKinnon John MacRory, Vic Lauchlan, Calum MacGuiness, John MacGuiness.

On the voyage across the Sound of Sleat, Charles and his friends were challenged by a party of armed militia in a boat. Fortunately, the sea was too rough for the militia to come close enough for a thorough inspection. At daybreak, Charles' boat landed at Mallaigvaig on the northern shores of the Morar peninsula.

Charles was now feeling unwell. The many deprivations he had endured during the previous few weeks had taken their toll. His skin was emaciated with scurvy. He was still suffering from dysentry. He was tormented by lice.

Charles and his party had no idea which of the local people they could trust. It was obviously far too risky to seek shelter and accommodation from people they did not know. No matter where seven strangers might have lodged, their presence would have attracted attention very quickly. Not knowing where to go,

they just stayed out in the open for three days and nights. This state of limbo could not continue for much longer. It was crucial that they should seek better accommodation. Hoping to find someone they could trust, Old MacKinnon went among the local populace.

On one of these sorties, Old MacKinnon came across Old Clanranald, who, on the way back to Benbecula from his excursion to Fort William, was staying at Scothouse on the opposite shore of Loch Nevis. Old Clanranald was now very depressed, having seen what the clansfolk had suffered on Charles' account. In the circumstances, Old MacKinnon did not tell Old Clanranald about Charles' present whereabouts and predicament.

On 8 July, the fugitives decided to look for a cave. Old MacKinnon and John MacGuinness went to search on land. The others set off by boat to reconnoitre the south shore of Loch Nevis.

Mallaigvaig

With John MacKinnon at the tiller, Charles sat hidden under a plaid between MacKinnon's legs. As they rowed close to the shore, their oars accidently struck a moored boat. Disturbed by the noise, five militiamen suddenly appeared on the shore, and interrogated them. On learning that John and his crew had come from Skye, the militia ordered the boat to land. Instantly, John decided to ignore the order. Taking up an oar himself, he urged his men to row on as fast as they could.

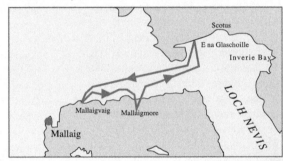

Charles' route on Loch Nevis

The bay at Mallaigmore

Immediately, the militia boarded their own boat, and set out in pursuit. During the chase, Charles panicked. He became very agitated, and objected to John assuming command. He demanded to be set ashore, and had to be restrained from leaping into the shallow water. From the bottom of the boat, he continually insisted on knowing how close their pursuers were. He protested when John ordered his men to fire if the militia came too close. However, John disregarded Charles' hysteria.

A small bay near Sron Raineach, close to the landing place

'And then my lads, be sure to take an aim, mark well and there is no fear. We will be able to manage these rogues if we come to engage them.'

Fortunately, there was no need for such drastic measures, John 'so animated his fellow-tuggers that they outrowed their blood-thirsty pursuers '.

With the militia still following, Charles and his companions landed, and took cover in the trees at the water's edge. While Charles and John ran up the hillside, the others waited in hiding to repel the enemy. The militia saw the dangers of trying to land, and gave up the chase. Watching them retreat, John made peace with Charles, and apologised for usurping Charles' authority. In return, Charles congratulated John on the escape. He excused his own behaviour by explaining that he would rather have fought for his life on shore than have been taken prisoner on board the boat.

For the next three hours, they all rested on the hill, contemplating the encounter with the enemy. It was obvious more than ever that they needed help, if they were to avoid further such dangers.

Gazing over Loch Nevis, they could pick out Scothouse on the far shore. As they knew Old Clanranald was staying there, they decided to approach him straight away. They rowed the three miles to Eilean na Glaschoille, a little island in Inverie Bay. John then continued alone to the mainland.

View across Loch Nevis from the south

John found Old Clanranald in the garden of the house. On seeing John approach, Old Clanranald tried to avoid the meeting by escaping into the house, but John caught him by the coat, before he could disappear. The embarrassed old man began to bluster.

'O!, Mr Mackinnon, is this you? I did not know you. How do you do? It is not easy to know people that come to visit us now.'

John's reply was sarcastic.

'Indeed it is hard nowadays to distinguish friends from foes. But I come as a friend, Clan, and have something to impart to you, if you will please to take a turn with me.'

After a few preliminaries, John came to the point.

'I am come from the Prince, who is not very far off from hence, and desires to know from you into whose hands he is now to be put, for that he will think himself safe with any person of persons you will recommend. He desires me likewise to tell you that he wants not to see you, or that you should run any personal risk on his account, as you did not join him in person, but that

Eilean na Glaschoille

you'll name any one with whom you think he will be safe.'

The old man now revealed his demoralised state of mind. He was no longer the brave stalwart who had helped Charles so daringly before.

'What muckle devil has brought him to this country again? For a second destruction to it no doubt, as the troops on hearing of his motions, will be sure to follow him fast and raze us all to the ground, leaving us nothing that they can either carry off or destroy.'

'It is truly astonishing,' said John, 'to hear a gentleman like you, Clan, talk at such a rate, when you know the Prince to be in the utmost danger, and, therefore, that he stands as much in need of faithful care and assistance as ever. To whom can he go for sanctuary in distress but to friends? And must he not move about from place to place, as shall be judged most fit, for to keep him out of the hands of his enemies who are continually hunting after him? I tell you over again that he expressly desires you may not run any risk whatsoever in your own person, not even by looking him in the face, but that you may name to me any person in whose hands you would judge him to be safe. It is very hard if you will not do that much for him in his greatest danger.'

'I tell you, Mr Mackinnon,' said Clanranald, 'I know of no person into whose hands I can put him. But if my advice or opinion can be of any use, it is that you should directly return with him from whence you came and land him speedily in the Island of Rona.'

'Indeed,' said John, 'I would as soon give him instantly up to the troops as do any such thing as you advise. For you know, Clan, as well as I do, that Rona being a little grass island not a single goat or sheep could escape a search on it, much less a man. If this the best advice or opinion you have to give, Clan, you had better keep it to yourself, for the following of it would be to throw the Prince directly into the hands of his enemies. I plainly see you are resolved not to do the smallest service to the Prince in his greatest distress, and that you want only to be rid of him, therefore you shall have no more trouble about him. But remember, Sir, that I will honestly inform him of every word that has pass'd between you and me on this subject, be the consequence what it will.'

On hearing John's devastating report, Charles was philosophical.

'Well, Mr Mackinnon, there is no help for it. We must do the best we can for ourselves.'

Under the cover of darkness, the party rowed back across Loch Nevis. On meeting up again with Old MacKinnon, they decided seek help elsewhere. The obvious direction was south to Borrodale. Surely, Charles' old friends there would help. Leaving the four boatmen behind, Charles, with Old MacKinnon and John MacKinnon set off.

14
8 - 10 JULY
MORAR to BORRODALE

The various movements between 8 and 10 July

The Enemy

Soon after returning home, the men who ferried Charles to Skye were rounded up by the troops. Under flogging, Lauchlan MacMurrich confessed to helping Charles, so Fergussone now had all the details of Charles' escape to Skye.

On 8 July, 1,500 troops landed on the Trotternish peninsular close to Monkstadt. Immediately, Lady Margaret's house was searched from top to bottom. Fergussone went to interrogate Kingsburgh. Flora MacDonald was summoned from her mother's house at Armadale.

As soon as the troops landed, Lady Margaret destroyed the much treasured, but incriminating, letter from Charles. She also convincingly denied any knowledge of Charles' landing on Skye. With Lieutenant MacLeod able to corroborate her alibi for the day of Charles' arrival, there was no material evidence against her.

Before confronting Kingsburgh, himself, Fergussone enticed Kingsburgh's dairymaid on board the *Furnace*, and tricked her into revealing the whole story of Charles' stay at Kingsburgh nine days previously. Thus, Fergussone had the upper hand, when he subsequently interrogated Kingsburgh and his family.

Kingsburgh openly admitted having Flora and her maid as house-guests. However, he feigned total ignorance of Charles. Despite Fergussone's bullying, the whole family stuck to this story. Eventually, Kingsburgh's wife was provoked into a very defiant outburst. Looking Fergussone straight in the face, she said. 'If Captain Ferguson is to be my judge, then God have mercy upon my soul.' When Fergussone asked the reason for this statement, she answered, 'Why, Sir, the world belies you if you be not a very cruel, hard-hearted man; and indeed I do not like to come through your hands.' Unaffected by this remark, Fergussone replied that people should not believe all that the world says. He continued to play the Kingsburghs along, and asked where Flora and 'the person along with her in woman's cloaths' slept'. Kingsburgh replied, 'I know in what room Miss MacDonald herself lay, but where the servants are laid when in my house, I know nothing of that matter, I never enquire anything about it. My wife is the properest person to inform you about that.'

Fergussone then 'had the impertinence' to ask whether or not she had laid the young Pretender and Miss MacDonald in one bed.

'Sir,' she said, 'whom you mean by the young Pretender, I shall not pretend to guess; but I can assure you it is not the fashion in the Isle of Sky to lay the mistress and the maid in the same bed together.'

Unimpressed by this indignation, Fergussone demanded to see the rooms in which these lodgers had slept. On being taken there, he noted dryly that 'it was pretty remarkable that the room in which the maid had slept seem's to look better that the one where the mistress had been laid; and this behoved to confirm him in the belief that it was the young Pretender in women's cloaths who had been along with Miss MacDonald'.

In desperation, Kingsburgh's daughter now tried her hand at pulling the wool over Fergussone's eyes. She said, 'it could not be the person he meant in women's cloaths, for that she had heard Flora's made ask for a bottle of water in Erse.'

Fergussone replied, 'This confirms me more and more in my opinion, for I have often heard that a fellow went to Rome some years agoe on purpose to teach the young Pretender the Erse language.' Inevitably, Fergussone finally took Kingsburgh into custody ready for further interrogation by General Campbell.

On receiving the summons to Portree, Flora and her friends destroyed the letter that her stepfather had given as permission to make the crossing from Benbecula. Then, they hastily concocted a story about how she came across 'Betty Burke'.

'... she said she had seen a great lusty woman, who came to the boatside as she was going on board and begged to have a passage, saying she was a soldier's wife. Her request was granted, and when she landed in Sky, she went away, thanking Miss for her favour. Miss added withal that she knew nothing of what became of her afterwards.'

The troops were not deceived, and Flora was taken into custody.

The Morar estuary

The Friends

O'Sullivan and Dumont   Out in the Atlantic, *Le Hardi Mendiant* was in difficulties. On the day before she was due to rendezvous with O'Neil, the appearance of an enemy man-of-war forced her to keep well out to sea. Then, she ran into a violent gale, that caused her serious damage, and blew her well north of Cape Wrath. When they were two days late for the meeting with O'Neil, O'Sullivan and Dumont decided to sail to Norway, from where they would organise another rescue attempt.

The Prince

The Prince's companions: Old MacKinnon and John MacKinnon

Charles and his two friends made very slow progress, as they walked through the night. Charles was feeling very unwell, and had difficulty in walking more than a short distance. While passing a shieling, they were alarmed by the approach of another party coming along the same path in the opposite direction. In order to avoid the Prince being recognised, they decided to pass Charles off as a servant.

Under the cover of darkness, John hurriedly tied a handerchief round Charles' head, folded a plaid, and threw it, together with a knapsack, over Charles' shoulder. The ploy worked, and Charles was not recognised. Nevertheless, his poor condition drew attention and comment from the other party. John had to explain that it was his plan to leave this 'servant' with MacDonald of Morar, a short distance along the road.

After a drink of milk at the shieling, they continued to the next, where again they had to stop to refresh Charles with more milk. Just ahead, was the River

The River Morar near the crossing place

Morar, wide, deep and fast flowing. As the ford was not easy to see, the MacKinnons hired a guide at the shieling.

John saw that the crossing would be too much for Charles in his poor state of health. He therefore asked the guide to carry the sick 'servant' across the river on his back. The guide took the request as an insult, and reacted arrogantly. At the same time, he showed that he did not suspect that the sick man was anything other than the lowly servant, he was said to be.

'The deel be on the back he comes or any fellow of a servant like him. But I'll take you on my back, sir, if you please, and carry you safely through the ford.'

'No, no, by no means,' said John. 'If the lad must wade, I'll wade along with him and help him, lest any harm should happen to him.'

John supported Charles, as they braved the river to the other side.

In the early hours of the morning, they came to a bothy, where Allan MacDonald of Morar and his family were now living. Their burnt-out house was nearby. John went into the bothy alone to rouse Morar. After introducing the visitors to his household, Morar sent his children and servants back to bed. Morar's wife was Lochiel's daughter, and had met Charles previously. This new meeting was an emotional and tender occasion, with the lady bursting into a flood of tears. Morar was eager to help, and after giving his visitors a meal of cold salmon, he led them to a nearby cave. Morar then went in search of Young Clanranald, who, they all thought, would help, despite the attitude of his father.

When Morar returned ten hours later, his manner had changed completely. Gone was the eagerness to help. He now appeared cold-hearted, and, in an embarrassed way, was indifferent to the Prince and his party. When Morar said he had been unable to find Young Clanranald, Charles asked Morar to help them alone. However, Morar told them

he could do nothing to help. Neither did he know of any one who could.

At this, Charles was understandably angry.

'This is very hard. You was very kind yesternight, Morar, and said you could find out a hiding place proof against all the search of the enemies forces, and you now say you can do nothing at all for me. You can travel to no place but what I will travel to. No eatables or drinkables can you take, but what I can take a share along with you, and be well content with them, and even pay for them. When Fortune smiled upon me and I had pay to give, I then found some people ready enough to serve me, but now that fortune frowns on me and I have no pay to give, they forsake me in my necessity.'

John MacKinnon joined in the rebuke.

'I am persuaded, Morar, though you deny it, you have met with your betters and gotten bad counsel, otherwise you would not have changed your mind so much as you have done in so short a time. For yesterday you was as hearty as one could have wished to do everything for the preservation of the Prince, whose situation is just the same as when you left us; and as there is no change at all in his circumstances, why this sudden change in your resolutions?'

Morar continued to deny that he had met Young Clanranald, or been influenced by anyone. However, the MacKinnons did not believe him. They were now convinced that the whole family of the Clanranald chief was against helping Charles, and that Morar's change of heart was a result of having received orders from a higher level.

Charles became desperate.

'O God Almighty! Look down upon my circumstances and pity me; for I am in a most melancholy situation. Some of those who joined me at first and appeared to be fast friends, now turn their backs upon me in my greatest need, and some of those again who refused to join me and stood at a distance are among my best friends. For it is remarkable that those of Sir Alexander MacDonald's following have been most faithful to me in my distress, and contributed greatly to my preservation. I hope Mr Mackinnon you will not desert me too and leave me in the lurch, but that you'll do all for my preservation you can.'

Old MacKinnon was distressed by the last remark, believing that it was addressed to him. Weeping, he replied.

'I never will leave your Royal Highness in the day of danger, but will, under God, do all I can for you, and go with you wherever you order me.'

'O no,' said the Prince, 'that is too much for one of your advanced years, Sir. I heartily thank you for your readiness to take care of me as I am well satisfied of your zeal for me and my cause. But one of your age cannot well hold out with the fatigues and dangers I must undergo. It was to your friend John here, a stout young man, I was addressing myself.'

'Well then,' said John, 'with the help of God I will go through the wide world with your Royal Highness, if you desire me.'

After further discussion, Charles resolved to go to Aeneas MacDonald of Borrodale. Although Borrodale was also of Clanranald, he had always been one of Charles most loyal friends. Charles therefore felt confident that he would help. Charles then asked Morar if he would, at least, do as much as providing a guide. Morar offered his own young son. After ascertaining that the boy did not know whom he would be guiding, Charles agreed to this suggestion.

Charles also wanted to find out what was happening in the enemy's headquarters at Fort Augustus, and asked Morar if he could send someone to find out. Morar suggested a local pedlar who went there occasionally. When Charles gave Morar a guinea to pay the pedlar, Morar protested that a whole guinea was too much. At this remark, Charles could not restrain himself from a scornful reply.

'Well then, Sir, if you think so, give him the one half and keep the other to yourself.'

It was now decided that Old MacKinnon would stay with Morar, while John and the Prince would set off late at night.

As Borrodale House was now a burnt-out ruin, the Borrodale family was staying in a bothy. John and Charles arrived just before daybreak. On being roused from his bed by John's calls, Borrodale appeared at the entrance, his blankets thrown around him. John learned that Borrodale had heard no recent news about the Prince.

'What would you give for a sight of him?,' said John.

'Time was,' replied Borrodale, ' when I would have given a hearty bottle to see him safe, but since I see you, I expect to hear some news of him.'

John then revealed the momentous purpose of his unexpected visit.

'Well, then, I have brought him here, and will commit him to your charge. I have done my duty. Do you yours.'

The impact of such a bombshell can only be imagined. Borrodale was struck with consternation, panic and joy. After a few speechless moments, he was able to reply.

'I am glad of it, and shall not fail to take care of him. I shall lodge him so secure that all the forces in Britain shall not find him out.'

At first, Charles was reluctant to enter the bothy, because he now knew that one of Borrodale's sons had been killed at Culloden. He approached Borrodale's wife with tears in his eyes, and asked if she could endure the sight of one who had been the cause of so much distress to her and her family.

'Yes,' she said, 'Though all my sons had perished in your service, for in doing so they had only done their duty.'

The bothy was a far cry from the spacious house that had been proudly used to accommodate Charles just less than a year ago. It comprised one gloomy room, with a poor table and only one chair. There were two beds of straw on the ground.

Later, Charles was taken to a cave on the shore where there is 'a rocky precipice so steep that some parts of it are almost perpendicular; that in a cleft or between two rocks of said precipice, there was a bothie or hut, so artfully contrived with the grassy side of the turf outward, that it exactly represented a natural green brae'.

After a short rest, John MacKinnon took his leave. According to tradition, Charles presented him with a recipe as a parting gift. It was for a drink based on whisky. It is said to be the liqueur now known as 'Drambuie'. As he left, John asked Charles 'if ever they might hope for the happiness of seeing him again'. Charles replied that 'if ever it pleased God that he should reach the Continent, though he should go and beg assistance of the Grand Turk, he would not suffer the usurper to sit easy or quiet on the throne'.

The cave at Borrodale

15
10 - 18 JULY
BORRODALE to GLEN FINNAN

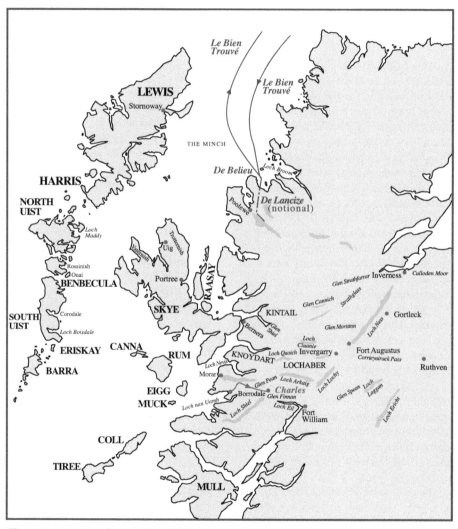

The various movements between 10 and 18 July

The Enemy

At his new headquarters in Lady Margaret's Macdonald's house, Campbell was now confident of success.

'I think as we have now fix'd him on Sky he cannot escape if we can but prevent his getting to the continent.'

(10 July, 1746)

When General Campbell interrogated Flora on board the *Furnace*, she confessed to having helped Charles. Having no idea about Charles' current whereabouts, she was unable to help Campbell in his searches. Much impressed by her bravery and dignity, Campbell gave Fergussone orders for her 'to be used with the utmost respect'.

Kingsburgh told Campbell all that he knew, even down to the detail of the 'Betty Burke' dress. The interrogation took place in the presence of Macleod of Talisker, who, being an old friend of Kingsburgh's, knew that Kingsburgh often sang a song about a lady with green sleeves. Facetiously, Talisker enquired 'Had she greensleeves?' Kingsburgh was then put on board the *Furnace*. However, Sir Alexander, who had just been sent back to Monkstadt by Cumberland, persuaded Campbell that Kingsburgh should not be put in irons.

Acting on Kingsburgh's revelations, the redcoats poured on to Raasay. At the same time, the helpless residents of Raasay were subjected to another onslaught of ravage, rape and pillage. On 17 July, the troops finally caught Malcolm MacLeod, hiding in a cave on the island.

Fergussone set off with a force of 200 men to the MacKinnon country. At Elgol, John MacKinnon and the four boatmen were arrested immediately they returned in the early hours of 11 July. Fergussone had John MacGuinness stripped, tied to a tree, and whipped 'till the blood gushed out at both his sides'.

John was cross-examined by General Campbell, in the presence of Fergussone, Talisker, and Campbell of Skipness, who was General Campbell's son. John insisted that he did not know Charles' current whereabouts. He confessed to having taken Charles to Morar, but maintained that he had taken the Prince only the distance of a gunshot from the shore, and had left him to be guided further by a little boy they had met accidentally. John was asked why he had not given Charles up to the troops. In reply, John tried to mislead his interrogators as to Charles' physical condition.

'It was never in my power, Sir, to deliver him up, for Your Excellency very well knows I am a man of no power, and therefore could not command the assistance of any men in such an enterprise. As little durst I attempt it by myself, though my inclination had led me to it, for he is able to tie two of me, neck and heel at any time.'

'Tie two of you, Mr Mackinnon! Why, he must be a dreadful young fellow. He must be remarkably strong indeed,' said the General.

'Truly,' said John, 'I can assure Your Excellency that he is as strong and nimble a young man as any one in all the Highlands of Scotland, and the fatigues he undergoes plainly prove him to be so.'

'By all the accounts I have had of him,' said the General, 'I believe him to be a pretty young fellow indeed. But, pray, Mr Mackinnon, was he not troubled with a bloody flux when among your hands, as I have heard the like from others? And in that case he would have been easily subdued.'

'No,' said John, 'He was in health when with me, and stout and bold as a lion.'

Campbell then asked John if he had not

been tempted by the £30,000 reward. John replied defiantly.

'To be plain with Your Excellency, what a base unworthy fellow it would have been in me who had been in his service, had received his pay, and broke his bread to have given him up! I would not have done it for the whole world. And had I done it, I daresay Your Excellency would have looked upon me as monster and wretch.'

Campbell was plainly impressed by such a brave response, and said so to his companions.

'Gentlemen, let us lay to heart what Captain Mackinnon has just now said, and let us determine from honour and conscience, and then surely we should applaud his conduct. For should any of us chance to be in the service of one, to follow his fortunes and to receive his pay and let us only suppose that such an one should be reduced to necessity of shifting for himself by the fate of war, and that he should come to us and throw himself into our arms, desiring to do anything with him he pleased, would not our behaviour in such a case be the same with Captain Mackinnon's? To be sure it should be such.'

After murmers of general agreement from his colleagues, Campbell continued.

'Pray, Captain Fergussone, fill up a glass for me to drink to Captain Mackinnon, and fill up another for him.'

To John's immense satisfaction, the barbaric Fergussone was then obliged to stand, and serve John, as he was sitting. Fergussone was later ordered to give him a good bed.

The news of Charles' escape to the mainland was speedily taken to Cumberland at Fort Augustus. On 13 July, he dispatched a force of 1,500 men to the coast. The plan was to trap Charles in the Arisaig peninsula. Some of the troops were to sail with Campbell into Loch Nevis, and then march up Glen Dessary to the head of Loch Arkaig. Scott was to take another force to Loch nan Uamh, and march from Glen Finnan over to Loch Arkaig to join up with Campbell's men. From there, a cordon of troops was to be thrown right across the Arisaig peninsula. There was also to be an outer cordon stretching along the Great Glen from Inverness to Fort William. The aim was to contain Charles within the cordons, and flush him out with more troops moving inland from the coast.

The Friends

The French When *Le Lévrier Volant* returned to France, the French Navy Minister, Le Comte de Maurepas, regarded the failure of its mission as being Charles' own fault.

> 'It seems certain that the Stuart Prince is in one or other of the small islands of the north of Scotland. But he is so well concealed from his enemies and from those who would help him, that both seek him with the same lack of success.'

For the next rescue attempt, the French now recruited Dumay, from *Le Lévrier Volant*, together with Lynch, O'Byrne, Warren and Sheridan, all of whom had escaped from Scotland after previous missions. Two expeditions, each with two ships, were to go to the west and east coasts of Scotland respectively.

O'Sullivan and Dumont When O'Sullivan arrived at Bergen, he took up residence in the house of the French consul. There, he decided to rescue Charles by sailing back to the Outer Isles in a ship belonging to a neutral country. The arrangements were made in great secrecy. Even the consul was not told of O'Sullivan's real purpose. O'Sullivan deceived the consul into thinking that Charles had escaped to Sweden, and that the aim of the proposed return to Scotland was to rescue some French officers. The consul agreed to charter a ship, load it with cargo, and secure the necessary passports. O'Sullivan then sent a thinly coded letter to France, giving news of Charles, and conveying his plans for this attempt. In the following extract, the term 'Isle of Heaven' is deliberately used instead of Isle of Skye, and 'Associate' refers to Charles.

'The ship *Le Hardi Mendiant* is a very small, one masted vessel, and in consequence without any defence. It would therefore not be prudent to risk in her any merchandise of value. I have proposed therefore, for greater safety, to charter a Dutch ship from here, at whatever cost, and to load her with planks which we are certain to sell in Scotland, in Ireland or in France, to have passports from here to these different places, and that I should go as super-cargo. To touch first at the Isle of Heaven where my most valuable depot is, and embark, if its locality has not been changed and thereafter to do as shall please my Associate.'

(15 July, 1746)

Two or three days later, the privateer, *Le Comte de Lowenthal*, arrived in Bergen after taking four other ships as prizes en route. Being a trusted acquaintance of O'Sullivan and Dumont, her commander, Captain Foyn, was let into their secret. He joined in the inspection of the ship being prepared by the French consul. Unfortunately, Dumont and Foyn both considered the ship to be unseaworthy. Foyn also warned O'Sullivan and Dumont that the

French consul could not be trusted. Indeed, Foyn thought the French consul would reveal the true purpose of O'Sullivan's expedition to his English counterpart. The arrangement with the French consul was immediately cancelled, so O'Sullivan began to look for a ship elsewhere.

De Lancize and de Belieu On 12 July the two Frenchmen were delighted and relieved to see *Le Bien Trouvé* sail back into Loch Broom. Anguier had also had second thoughts about de Lancize and de Belieu trying to find Charles on their own. Anguier had therefore decided to return prematurely to Loch Broom to see if the two men had actually left.

Once de Lancize and de Belieu were re-united with their ship, it was decided to re-plan the missions to Loch Arkaig. De Lancize, with two cadets, Berar and Dudepet, would now travel there on foot using local guides. De Belieu and another cadet, de Nangis, would make their way by boat. Meanwhile, *Le Bien Trouvé*, would cruise out in the Atlantic, and come back to meet the two returning shore parties in ten days.

After the ship had left, de Lancize and his cadets set off with Alexander MacLeod as guide. De Belieu and de Nangis met immediate disaster, when their rowing boat was intercepted by HMS *Furnace* at the mouth of Loch Broom.

The Prince

The Prince's companions: Aeneas MacDonald of Borrodale, John MacDonald, and Ranald MacDonald

In Borrodale, Charles now felt more secure than he had for some days. He also had the opportunity to take stock of his situation, and consult other people. In particular, he sent Borrodale's son, John, with a letter seeking the help of Alexander MacDonald of Glen Aladale, who lived just a few miles to the south-east of Borrodale.

As a major in the army, Glenaladale had been very close to Charles. In fact, he had become one of Charles' favourite and most trusted officers. At Culloden, he had been wounded three times, and was still not properly recovered. Although his wife and five young children were unwell and in great distress, his sense of duty to Charles forced him to answer the call.

When news of the MacKinnons' capture reached the Prince on 13 July, it caused immediate consternation. Would they divulge Charles' whereabouts under interrogation and torture? It was now essential to leave immediately. Hence, Borrodale and his other son, Ranald, took Charles to the remote MacLeod's Cove, high up in a precipice some four miles to the east. Borrodale then returned home to meet Glenaladale, and led him to MacLeod's Cove.

On 16 July, Borrodale received a letter from his son-in-law, Angus MacEachine, who had sheltered Charles on his journey from Loch Arkaig to Borrodale in April. The letter carried news that the redcoats now suspected Charles to be in Borrodale. MacEachine also offered to conceal Charles once again at Meoble. Accordingly, Ranald was sent to prepare this new hide-out.

The next day, John MacDonald was sent back to Borrodale to determine the enemy's latest movements. On Loch nan Uamh, he 'visibly saw the whole coast surrounded by ships-of-war and tenders, as also the country by other military forces'.

Loch nan Uamh at Borrodale

On hearing this news, Charles immediately decided that it was too risky to stay at MacLeod's Cove any longer. Without waiting for Ranald to return, he set off for MacEachine's refuge, guided by Glenaladale, Borrodale, and John MacDonald. At Coire Beinn nan Cabar, they encountered MacEachine on his way to meet them. They must have been very surprised to learn from him that Young Clanranald was waiting to hide Charles at a safe place a few miles away. As it was too late in the day to reach Young Clanranald, they pressed on to MacEachine's refuge, while Borrodale was dispatched to bring some supplies.

There, they were joined by Glenaladale's brother, also called John MacDonald. He told them that six men-of-war under the command of General Campbell had anchored in Loch Nevis. In order to determine what was happening there, two local men were sent from Loch Morar to Loch Nevis. Meanwhile, Borrodale returned with the news that Captain Scott had arrived with a force just to the south of them.

As the way to Clanranald's hiding place

was also cut off, Charles decided to move inland to keep ahead of the redcoats. He also realised that the present party was too big, and would attract attention. Hence, Borrodale and Angus MacEachine were left behind, while Glenaladale, with his brother and Borrodale's son, conducted Charles eastwards along the ridge on the south side of Loch Beoraid.

At midday, they rested on Sgurr a Mhuidhe, where Glenaladale's brother was sent on to find out what was happening in Glen Finnan. Before he left, they all arranged to meet again at ten o'clock at the summit of Sgurr nan Coireachan, on the other side of the glen to their north.

Charles, Glenaladale and Young Borrodale followed along the ridge, and, by two o'clock, had reached the hill, Fraoch-bheinn. Here, they came across some of Glenaladale's tenants driving their cattle away from the troops. While Glenaladale went to talk with his tenants, Charles and Young Borrodale kept their distance, taking the opportunity to rest.

The drovers told Glenaladale that

Loch Beoraid from the west

Sgurr nan Coireachan from Sgurr a Mhuide

there were troops mustering in Glen Finnan. Also, there were now five hundred or more troops at the head of Loch Arkaig. As the troops arrived, the residents were leaving. Glenaladale was particularly interested to learn that Donald Cameron of Glen Pean, the other man who had sheltered the Prince on the way from Culloden, had moved with his family to a hill not far away.

With the troops now directly in front of them, Charles had to change plan. Accordingly, Glenaladale sent one of his tenants back to Glen Finnan to recall his brother. He also sent another for Cameron of Glen Pean to guide them.

The hard day had taken its toll upon Charles. Still suffering from his sickness, he was utterly exhausted in the extreme heat. Near Fraoch-bheinn, his condition was pitied by a woman, who believed him to be Glenaladale's servant. She milked one of her cows, and brought him the milk. In great consternation, Charles feigned a headache, and covered his head with a handkerchief. The crisis was saved by Glenaladale, who, thanking the woman for her kindness, led her away from Charles.

Eventually, the messenger returned from Glen Finnan, without having met Glenaladale's brother. He reported that a hundred Argylshire militia were at the foot of the very hill, where they now were. At this news, Charles decided to leave for Sgurr nan Coireachan, without waiting for Gleanpean or Glenaladale's brother.

Sgurr Thuilm (on left), Streap (on right) from Fraoch-bheinn

16
18 - 19 JULY
GLEN FINNAN to LOCH ARKAIG

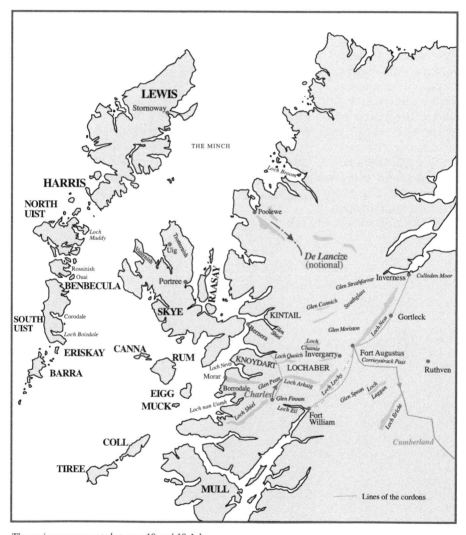

The various movements between 18 and 19 July

The Enemy

On 18 July, the Duke of Cumberland left Fort Augustus for the war in Flanders. His successor as Commander-in-Chief for Scotland was Lord Albemarle.

On the Arisaig peninsula, the cordons were now in place. The inner cordon, comprising some two thousand men, started at Loch Eil, and stretched unbroken to the head of Loch Arkaig. It then continued northwards as far Loch Hourn. The soldiers were placed within calling distance of each other. Over the whole length, there were seventeen camps, from which officers patrolled the cordon every quarter of an hour to ensure that their men were on watch.

Lord Albemarle

The Prince

The Prince's companions: Alexander MacDonald of Glen Aladale, John MacDonald (Glenaladale's brother) and John MacDonald (Borrodale's son).

In the gathering dusk, Glenaladale and Young Borrodale led the weary Charles back along the ridge. They descended to the east end of Loch Beoraid, and entered Coire Odhar Mor. As they toiled upwards by the stream, they entered thick cloud.

Round about eleven o'clock, they caught sight of a figure descending towards them in the mist.

Immediately, Glenaladale motioned his two companions to stand back,

Coire Odhar Mor

while he went to meet the newcomer. To his amazement and delight, it was none other than Donald Cameron of Glen Pean, who, having received the message sent earlier in the afternoon, was on his way to the Prince.

While they all rested to eat some oatmeal and butter, Glenpean told them that soldiers had been converging on the head of Loch Arkaig for the last two days. In addition to the forces from Loch Nevis and Glen Finnan in the west, five hundred redcoats, together with Munro and MacKay highlanders, had arrived from the east.

It was now necessary to find out exactly where the troops were disposed. Glenpean decided that they should go the summit of Sgurr Thuilm, where they would be able to observe the troops at the head of Loch Arkaig. He also knew that this mountain had been thoroughly searched that day. It was unlikely to be searched again very soon.

In the mist and darkness, Glenpean led the way 'through roads almost impassable even in daylight' to the summit of Sgurr nan Coireachan. They continued eastwards along the ridge, reaching Sgurr Thuilm round about four in the morning.

They could easily see great bonfires lighting the terrain below. There were four camps, one to their right in Gleann a' Chaorainn, two directly ahead on the plain at the head of Loch Arkaig, and one to their left. As day broke, they were able to discern a line of troops strung out across the whole valley below them. The fugitives were well and truly hemmed in. Now, they could not move anywhere in the daylight.

During the day, Charles slept while his friends kept watch. For food, they had only the remains of the oatmeal. Fortunately, the weather treated them kindly. As Glenpean had predicted, the mountain was not searched again that day. They observed the activity below without interruption.

Loch Arkaig from Sgurr Thuilm

The ridge between Sgurr Thuilm and Sgurr nan Coireachan

Glenpean anxiously kept an eye on his cottage at Kinlocharkaig, and pointed out to Charles the Campbells in the act of plunder.

'Does your Royal Highness see you? Yonder are they driving away my cattle.'

'How many cattle may you have?' said the Prince; '500 or 400?'

'No, not so many,' replied Donald, 'only about two or 300.'

'Well,' said the Prince, 'I am sorry to see to this. But keep up a good heart, Donald; I hope to see you yet taking five for one from the Campbells.'

Glenpean now had 'the best evidence in Europe to prove the taking away of his cattle, as the Prince was looking on them being driven away by the enemy'.

At one point, there was great alarm when they spotted a solitary figure approaching along the ridge from Sgurr nan Coireachan. They all thought it might be the first of the soldiers moving inland to trap them.

To everyone's joy and relief, it was Glenaladale's brother. Fortunately, he had not come to any harm on his quest to Glen Finnan the previous day. On making his way back to Fraoch-bheinn, he had feared the worst when his friends were not there. However, he had kept to the original plan for the rendezvous on Sgurr nan Coireachan. Not finding anyone there, he had deduced correctly that they had continued along the ridge to Sgurr Thuilm.

As the day wore on, it became clear that there was only one reasonable plan to escape from the trap. Under cover of darkness, they had to descend to the cordon, and find a weak point, which they could breach. At nine'o'clock in the evening, they decided to start the descent, while there was still some light.

17
19 - 21 JULY
LOCH ARKAIG to LOCH HOURN

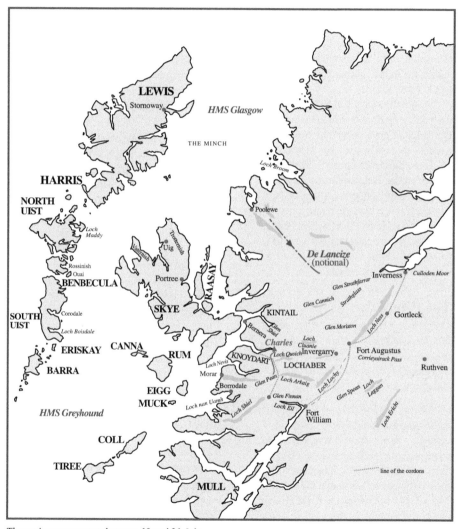

The various movements between 19 and 21 July

The Enemy

In his new post, Lord Albemarle decided to set up a network of agents and informers throughout the Highlands. Their job was to provide information about Charles, prominent Jacobites, and French rescue ships. Albemarle also decided to take a tough line with Barrisdale, who was not being very effective as an agent for the government. On 20 July, Barrisdale was given an ultimatum. If he did not produce results within one month, his pardon and privileges would be removed.

By now, the navy had been informed of the visit by *Le Bien Trouvé* to Loch Broom. On 19 July, Captain Fergussone sailed HMS *Furnace* there to investigate. In a short stay, his troops ransacked houses, and stole fifty head of cattle. Fergussone also acquired sufficient information to realise that the French ship was likely to return fairly soon. The next day, HMS *Glasgow* and HMS *Greyhound* were patrolling each end of the Minch in wait. Several other ships were also stationed near Loch Broom.

The Prince

The Prince's companions: Alexander MacDonald of Glen Aladale, John MacDonald (Glenaladale's brother), John MacDonald (Borrodale's son) and Donald Cameron of Glen Pean.

Having descended from Sgurr Thuilm, the fugitives approached the cordon in darkness. However, with so many troops concentrated at the head of Loch Arkaig, there was no possibility of breaking through there. They therefore skirted the foot of Monadh Gorm, crossed the River Dessary, and began to climb up the northern slopes of Glen Dessary.

To discover weak spots in the cordon, Charles and his friends had to crawl very close to the troops. These manoeuvres were extremely dangerous, because the enormous bonfires illuminated the land for yards around. Several times, they were so close to the cordon that they could hear the soldiers calling to each other. In one attempt to penetrate the cordon, they were surprised by an approaching patrol, but, by sheer good luck, they were able to avoid discovery by scrambling into a moss hole. Each time they tried to break through, their hopes were dashed by the vigilance of the enemy.

They could only follow the cordon down into Glen Kingie, where the cordon snaked westwards on the north side of the river, climbed the hillside on the right, and descended Coire Reidh to Loch Quoich. The fugitives kept a safe distance on the other side of the river. From the head of the glen, they climbed northwards to the summit of An Eag, where they could observe the fires in Coire Reidh. Here, they resigned themselves to the fact that they would not break through the cordon that night.

Now, they were extremely hungry. Over the last two days, they had eaten nothing but the small supply of uncooked oatmeal and butter. As only a few scraps remained, it was now essential to find food. Glenpean thought that they might be able obtain some from clansfolk who had taken refuge in the nearby Coire nan Gall. They decided to go there, and resume following the cordon the next night.

They reached Coire nan Gall about one o' clock in the morning. Finding the shiely huts abandoned, they had no alternative but to continue down the corrie without eating. One hour later, they stopped in 'a fast place in the face of a hill at the head of Lochqhaigh'. After a rest, Glenpean and Glenaladale's brother set off to find provisions. Meanwhile, Charles slept, while Glenaladale and Young

Borrodale kept guard. At daybreak, they were alarmed to see an enemy camp not very far away at the head of the loch. Nevertheless, they decided to stay where they were, rather than move further away.

Round about three in the afternoon, their friends returned with two small cheeses. They also reported that a hundred redcoats were searching the other side of the hill on which they were hiding. Despite the danger of being found, they remained in their hiding place until eight in the evening.

In the dusk, they climbed directly above their resting place to the top of Druim a Chosaidh. Looking down the other side of the ridge, 'they observed the fires of a camp directly in their front, which they could scarcely shun at Glenqhosy'. The fires were strung out from Loch Quoich along the whole length of Gleann Cosaidh, before disappearing into the distance down Glen Barrisdale. The only way forward now was down into Gleann Cosaidh, and through the cordon.

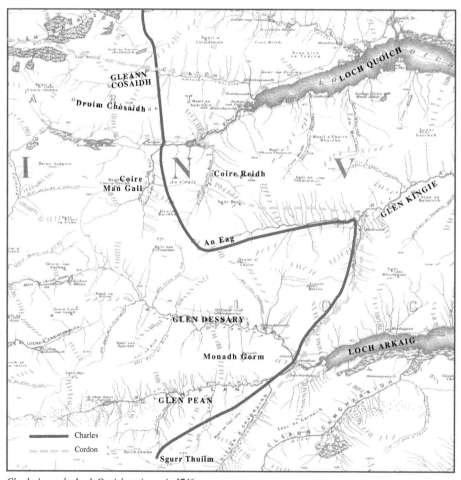

Charles' route by Loch Quoich, as it was in 1746

This descent nearly ended in disaster.

> 'Donald Cameron being guide was foremost,
> the Prince was after him, and I followed in his
> rear, and my brother and cousine after me, and
> crossing a small rivulet that gushed out of a
> spring, as I think, and glyded over a precpis at
> the very place we crossed it, Donald Cameron
> crossed first, the Prince next, and in crossing,
> missed a step, and 'tis altogether probable he
> would fall down the precipis, we took to be very
> high, if he had not been very full of life that
> I caught hold of one arm and Donald Cameron
> of the other and recovered him in a tryce.'

Fortunately, the Prince suffered no injury. They reached
the valley floor without further mishap.

In the shadows on the south bank, they followed the
cordon westwards to the head of the glen. Round about
two in the morning, Glenpean found a gully cutting across
the glen between two sentries. It looked possible to crawl
unseen along this gully to the other side of the cordon.
Glenpean thought the crossing 'was exceedingly
hazardous, but was the only place he could advise the
Prince to attempt'. Desperate for a way across, they
decided to try here.

Gleann Cosaidh

A gully at the head of Gleann Cosaidh

Glenpean decided that he should go along the gully alone first.

'If I get safe through and also return safe, then you may venture with greater security, and I shall be all the better fitted to conduct you.'

As he left, he complained that his nose was itching.

'O Sir, my nose is yuicking, which is a sign to me that we have great hazards and dangers to go through.'

The others peered after him, dreading to hear the shout or shot that would signal disaster. Eventually, Glenpean re-emerged, and beckoned everyone to follow. Nervously, they all crawled along the gully. On the other side, they scampered up the hill in the safety of the darkness.

Once out of the enemy's earshot, they stopped to catch their breath. Flushed with success, Charles joked with Glenpean.

'Well, Donald, how does your nose now?'

'It is better now,' answered Donald, 'but it still yuicks a little.'

'Ay, Donald,' replied the Prince. 'Have we still more guards to go through?'

Their route now lay up to the top of the ridge above them, and down the other side to Kinloch Hourn. Young Borrodale tells how they stopped just before daybreak.

'The Thyrd morning we arrived near the top of a high mountain near Lochhurn head and found a safe place to spend the day in a bit hollow ground, covered with long heather and brenches of jung birch bushes, where we all five of us lay down to rest, almost fainting for want of food; these severe tryals and circumstance drew many heavy sighs from his poor oppressed heart. I informed him then that I had a leepy of groaten meal wrapt up in a Nepkin in my pocket, which when I produced, made alwast alteration in counteinance of the whole of them. Come, come says he, let us in Gods name have a share; never was people in more need. I expect soon to meet with plenty; so I divided the whole of it between us five; and they began to chat and crak heartily, after our refreshment.'

18
21 - 23 JULY
LOCH HOURN to LOCH CLUANIE

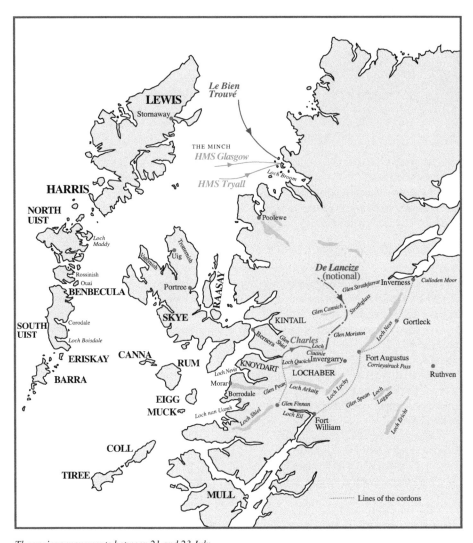

The various movements between 21 and 23 July

The Enemy

Having been in command for several days, Lord Albemarle wrote the first of his regular letters to Lord Newcastle, the Minister for War.

> 'I beg the Favour of Your Grace to assure His Majesty that I shall not leave this Place till the Hopes of securing the Pretender's Son are all over, and that I shall do all in my Power to effect the Orders left with me by the Duke, having nothing more in view than to execute the Trust reposed in me.'

> (22 July, 1746)

The Friends

The French It was now confirmed that the Colonel Richard Warren would be in overall command of the next expedition to rescue Charles. Warren was so overjoyed that he wrote a very effusive letter to Louis.

> 'I have compassed at last what in the present circumstances I `could desire. I part for Port Louis in a day or two. Thence I sail off with 2 frigatts and 2 more from Morlaix under my command in order join his Royal Highness the Prince and bring him back to France. These are my orders,which I hope in God I shall effectuate. None could be more suitable for my zeal and attachment. My Joy will be complete, if I find the choice of my person for so honoreable a comission is agreable to your Majesty.'

> (21 July, 1746)

O'Sullivan and Dumont In Bergen, O'Sullivan, with the aid of Captain Foyn, had now been able to charter another ship. However, it was not available for another two weeks.

Meanwhile, another French privateer, *Le Comte de Maurepas*, had arrived in port, and, like *Le Comte de Lowenthal*, it was under orders to try and find the Prince. O'Sullivan now saw the ideal opportunity to prevent further delay. At a special dinner party, he and Dumont persuaded the captains of the two privateers to sail their ships as escorts for *Le Hardi Mendiant* in a rescue mission that would leave in three days' time. If the attempt failed, he intended to return, and try again with the ship that he would be able to charter in two weeks.

Anguier Out in the Atlantic, Anguier in *Le Bien Trouvé* had encountered several ships of the Royal Navy, but his wily seamanship had kept his ship out of serious trouble. He was also able to continue on his way for the rendezvous with the shore party at Loch Broom. On 22 July, he was confronted by the two ships that were lying in wait, as he approached the loch. He was forced to escape to the open sea. The next day, Anguier tried again, only to be chased into the loch by the frigate, HMS *Glasgow*. Eventually, *Le Bien Trouvé* became trapped, when HMS *Tryall* blocked her in a narrow channel between two islands. Anguier was forced to surrender.

De Lancize Having parted from Alexander MacLeod, De Lancize, Berar and Dudepet had not reached Lochaber. They had just wandered from village to village, enquiring discretely where Charles might be found. Barrisdale heard of their arrival in one village, and led a party of troops to capture them. However, the Frenchmen managed to escape.

Dudepet had now become separated from the other two, and had fallen ill. He was about to give himself up. De Lancize, realising that he and Berar were too far away from Loch Broom to return on time for the planned rendezvous with *Le Bien Trouvé*, decided to continue with their mission to Lochaber.

The Prince

The Prince's companions: Alexander MacDonald of Glen Aladale, John MacDonald (Glenaladale's brother), John MacDonald (Borrodale's son) and Donald Cameron of Glen Pean.

Elated but exhausted, Charles and friends spent the whole of the day resting, well hidden in the hollow above Kinloch Hourn. They felt so secure that they moved about the hollow and to a nearby stream without crawling. They also talked to each other in normal voices. However, they did not dare to venture out in search of the much needed food.

Charles' thoughts now turned once again to the French rescue ship that, he now thought, would be at Poolewe.

Unfortunately, Glenpean did not know the way. Nevertheless, he thought there might be some local person, whom they could trust to lead them there. In the late afternoon, he set out with Glenaladale to find a new guide.

When they had gone only a few yards from the hollow, they were alarmed to see two army camps 'within a cannon shot' at the foot of the hill where they had rested. Immediately, they took cover, and watched the soldiers, about forty strong, driving some sheep into folds.

When Glenpean and Glenaladale crept back to the others with their news, Charles decided that they must move on without a guide. However, they 'durst not move till dark night, for fear of being discovered'.

They walked northwards up Glen Sgoireadail throughout the night. For Young Borrodale, it was 'the darkest night ever in my life I traveled'. At sunrise, they arrived in Glen Shiel, exhausted and desperately hungry. After a short rest, Glenaladale and Young Borrodale went off to obtain food, and recruit a guide to take them to Poolewe.

Kinloch Hourn from a hollow near the entrance to Coire Sgoireadail

Coire Sgoiraedail from Coire Shubh

In a nearby village, they were able to buy cheese and butter from a man, by the name of Gilchrist MacGrath. MacGrath also agreed to try and find a guide for them. He arranged to meet them later that afternoon a mile or so up the glen, where Charles and companions were presently waiting.

Glenaladale also encountered Donald MacDonald, an old acquaintance from the Prince's army. Donald had just fled from his home in Glen Garry, after his father had been shot by troops the day before. Without broaching the matter, Glenaladale decided that Donald might be trusted as the guide, if MacGrath failed to recruit a local from Glen Shiel.

When Glenaladale and Young Borrodale returned to the others, they all set about the food.

> 'Words cannot express the quantity we consumed of the buter and cheese at the time, though both kind exceeding salt.'

Instead of waiting for MacGrath by the track, they climbed up the steep side of the glen in search of a safe place. Eventually, they found an overhanging rock under which they could rest, hidden from view, and sheltered from the sun.

The resting place in Glen Shiel

As the day wore on, the five men began to suffer the combined effects of the heat and salty food.

> 'We ... were all seized with such a druth, that we were all like to perish before sunset.'

The nearest source of water was the River Shiel, about forty yards down the hill side. However, Charles refused to allow anybody to leave the hiding place, in case they attracted attention.

In the late afternoon, Glenpean began the long walk back home. Having brought Charles as far as he could, he now wanted to return to his wife and family.

Soon afterwards, Glenaladale recognised the figure of Donald MacDonald, walking along the glen back to Glen Garry. Not wishing to miss the chance of using him as a guide, Glenaladale went down to talk to him. Very quickly, he convinced himself that Donald was very suitable. Without revealing his motives, Glenaladale somehow persuaded Donald to delay his journey, and wait near at hand. On Glenaladale's advice, Charles agreed that Donald should be kept by, until they heard from Gilchrist MacGrath.

At sunset, they all descended to the river, and 'drank water at no allowance'. In the distance, they saw a young boy approaching from the village. When Glenaladale and Young Borrodale went to meet him, they discovered him to be the son of Gilchrist MacGrath, coming to report that his father had been unable to procure a guide. He also informed them that there had been a French ship at Poolewe, but it had now left.

The boy had also brought five pints of goat's milk, which Glenaladale bought for four shillings. In taking his leave, Glenaladale let the boy believe they would now return home.

As they drank the milk, Charles decided that it was useless to go to Poolewe. However, he decided that Donald MacDonald should be their guide anyway. Thus, the Glen Garry man was fetched, and introduced to the Prince.

Late at night, they all set off up Glen Shiel. After about a quarter of an hour, Glenaladale discovered that his purse was no longer hanging from his belt. Very quickly, he remembered opening it to pay for the milk. He also realised that he must have dropped it, while kilting his plaid. Since the purse contained all the money they had,

Glenaladale and Young Borrodale decided to go back and look for it. Meanwhile, the others left the track, and crossed the river to wait behind some bushes.

Glenaladale found the purse exactly where he thought it would be. However, it now contained only five shillings. An inner purse, containing forty louis d'or, belonging to the Prince, was missing. Obviously, the boy had taken the gold, so they decided seek him out.

On arriving at the village, they roused Gilchrist MacGrath from his sleep, and reported the matter to him. Enraged by what his son had done, MacGrath went into his house, grabbed his son fiercely by the arm, and threatened him with a rope.

'You damned scoundrel! This instant get these poor gentlemen's money, which I am certain is all they have to depend upon, or, by heavens, I'll hing you to that very tree you see this moment!'

Shivering with fear, the boy went to retrieve the money, which he had buried close to the house.

When Glenaladale and Young Borrodale returned to the Prince, they found him very anxious and agitated, because an army officer with three soldiers had just passed by, heading towards the village. Charles was therefore worried that they would apprehend his two friends returning. As the night was so clear, Charles had refused to let any of his companions run ahead of the soldiers with a warning of the danger. Fortunately, Glenaladale and Young Borrodale had chosen to return on the other side of the river. Consequently, they had missed the soldiers completely.

On resuming their journey up Glen Shiel, they walked the whole way without any further incident. By ten o'clock the next morning, they reached Strathcluanie, where they stopped in 'a fast place' on the hillside.

The likely place where Glenaladale dropped his purse

19
23 JULY - 2 AUGUST
LOCH CLUANIE to STRATHGLASS

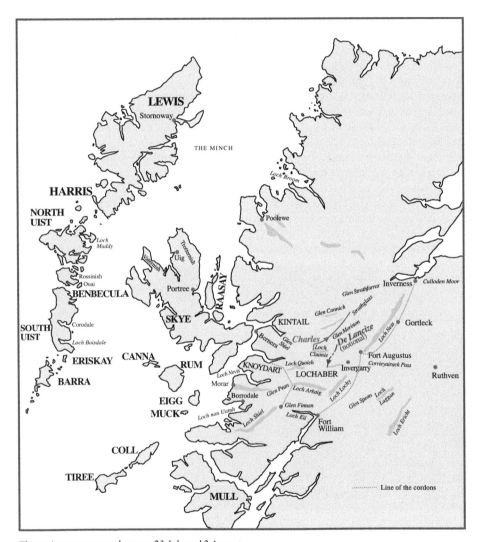

The various movements between 23 July and 2 August

The Enemy

From 23 to 25 July, the men that Cumberland had sent to scour the coast, arrived back at Fort William and Fort Augustus. As well as being empty-handed, they were suffering badly from the experience. Scott's men were 'vastly fatigued and almost naked'.

By now, Lord Albemarle realised that Charles had slipped through the net. As he gave orders for the cordons to be dismantled, Albemarle conveyed his disappointment to Lord Newcastle.

'I had a private information three Days ago, that he was gone from *Morer* last Wednesday was sennight before the Chain was entirely formed to *Lochaber*, where he was met by Loch Gary with seventy men armed who escorted him from thence to *Badenoch*. ..... Soon after I heard he was gone North through the Mac Kenzie's Country into Caithness; ..... I farther had intelligence that he was still in the Lands of Morer and Knoydart. But this is impossible, Colonel Conway and Capt Scott having scoured that whole country. The last Report that I had was, that he and two more went in a Boat from thence, before the King's Troops could get there, to the Long Island.'

(25 July, 1746)

Nevertheless, Albemarle was still full of determination.

'I neither shall leave off the Pursuit or Hopes of aprehending the Pretender's Son till I have orders to march into Quarters, notwithstanding the very bad weather we have within these three Days, or the want of Cloathing for our Men.'

(25 July, 1746)

A few days later, Albemarle admitted to Lord Newcastle, that he had completely lost track of Charles' whereabouts.

'Since my last, I have employed Friends (if any in these Hills) and Foes to procure me intelligence of the Pretender's Son; but have had none whatsoever for these past five days. He was then supposed, as I acquainted His Royal Highness last Post, to be lurking about *Loch Brume,* on the Western Coast, ill attended, hiding himself in the Day time and moving about from Place to Place at Night.'

(1 August, 1746)

At the coast, Campbell now had all the evidence he needed to implicate Old Clanranald in helping Charles. On 29 July, Old Clanranald was arrested.

The Friends

The French The arrangements to raise another rescue mission were in difficulties. No suitable ships were immediately available. In particular, *Le Mars* and *La Bellone* were still not repaired. The best that could be arranged was for just two ships, the 36-gun *L'Heureux* and the 30-gun *Le Prince du Conti,* to be ready in mid-August.

O'Sullivan On 24 July, O'Sullivan embarked on *Le Hardi Mendiant,* and joined *Le Comte de Maurepas* and *Le Comte de Lowendal* in the estuary at Bergen. Three days later, when the winds became favourable, all three ships set sail. O'Sullivan's plan was to make for Benbecula to see if O'Neil and Charles had arrived there, as previously arranged. If Charles was on the mainland, O'Sullivan hoped Old Clanranald would send messengers to Charles. Out at sea, strong winds twice blew the ships back round Cape Wrath towards Aberdeen.

While they waited for favourable winds, the two privateers engaged in piracy, and took three prizes. On one of their captures, they found newspapers containing alarming reports of O'Neil's capture, together with speculative, but frightening, accounts of Charles' dire predicament.

The Prince

The Prince's companions: Alexander MacDonald of Glen Aladale, John MacDonald (Glenaladale's brother), John MacDonald (Borrodale's son) and Donald MacDonald.

On the hillside at Strathcluanie, Charles and his friends rested throughout the day. Their refuge provided little protection from the incessant rain, and they were all soaked to the skin. At one stage, they heard gunshots not very far away, but saw no sign of any soldiers.

The calm warm evening brought the torment of midges. Although the highlanders could tolerate them with stoicism, the midges drove Charles to distraction. Wrapped from head to toe in his plaid, he lay covered with heather in a hollow. While his friends gathered around him, hoping to give further protection, he squirmed and groaned wretchedly.

By the end of the day, Charles had decided that he would go to Poolewe after all. This change of plan raised once again the problem of finding a guide, because Donald MacDonald did not know the way. Donald decided that they should seek the help of some of his friends, whom he knew to be hiding in Coire Dho, to the north of their present resting place.

When it was dark, they set off up the hillside on the north side of Loch Cluanie. By the time they reached the top, it was too dark to walk further. They waited for daylight in an open cave, which was so narrow that they all had to stand. Charles smoked his pipe in a vain attempt to warm himself. Round about three o'clock in the morning, Glenaladale's brother and Donald MacDonald went on to Coire Dho. It was arranged that Charles and the others would follow later for a rendezvous on a neighbouring summit.

Coire Dho

Four hours later, they met Donald, who reported meeting three of the men he wanted to find. After accepting an offer of food and shelter, Donald had come to bring Charles and the others to meet the men.

The three men, John MacDonald, Alexander MacDonald and Alexander Chisholm, had been led to believe that their early morning visitors were some fugitives including Young Clanranald. However, when John MacDonald, arrived later with a 'cogfull' of milk, he recognised the Prince, despite the 'whit cap, and an old Bonet above'. Instantly, the astonished John MacDonald 'changed collours, and turned red as blood'.

He was distressed at Charles' physical condition, and expressed his concern in Erse.

'I am sorry to see you in such a poor state, and hope if I live to see yet in a better condition, as I have seen you before at the head of your armie, upon the green of Glasgow: all I can doe is to continue faithfull to you while I live, and am willing to leave my wife and children, and follow you wherever you incline going.'

Taking the man by the hand, Charles replied.

'As you are a M'Donald, whom I allways found faithfull to my cause, I shall admit you to my smal partie, and trust myself to you.'

John MacDonald then offered accommodation in a cave in the nearby Coire Mheadhoin. The cave was under a large rock close to their own huts.

'The best water in the highland runen throu it, and a large void heather bed in it already made for your reception.'

With Charles in such a bad state of health, it required little persuasion for him to accept this offer, and postpone the trek to Poolewe. Soon, the fugitives found

The cluster of rocks containing the cave in Coire Mheadhoin

themselves 'as comfortably lodged as we had been in a Royal pallace'. Charles' hosts produced a meal of whisky, mutton, butter and cheese. That night 'his royal highness was lulled asleep with the sweet murmers of the finest purling stream that could be, running by his bedside, within the grotto'.

The three men in Coire Dho were in a band of seven Glen Moriston men who had served the Prince in the regiment commanded by MacDonnell of Glengarry. The band was led by a local farmer, Major Patrick Grant, and included Gregor MacGregor. There were also three brothers, Alastair, Donald and Hugh Chisholm, as well as two more brothers, John and Alexander MacDonald.

After watching the people of Glen Moriston suffer at the hands of the troops, these seven men had all taken an oath on their dirks against the Duke of Cumberland and his army.

'never to yield, but to die on the spot, never to give up their arms, and that for all the days of their lives'.

Subsequently, they had acquired a considerable reputation for their exploits. They had killed two out of a party of seven redcoats who were passing through Glen Moriston. They had murdered an informer sent from Strathspey to report on people in Glen Moriston. They had also ambushed a patrol of thirty soldiers to regain cattle stolen from Patrick Grant's father.

Impressed by their daring, Charles now invited these three desperadoes to join his service, but indicated that he had no need of the four absent members of their band. However, the three insisted that they were members of a group of seven, all under oath to serve each other. It was impossible for the three to leave their companions. They asked that Charles be prepared 'to trust himself to the other four as well as to them'. Wisely, he agreed.

Charles wanted his new recruits to maintain absolute security, and demanded that they should swear an oath.

'That their backs should be to God and their faces to the Devil; that all the curses the Scriptures did pronounce might come upon them and all their posterity if they did not stand firm to the Prince in the greatest dangers, and if they should discover to any person, man, woman or child, that the Prince was in their keeping till once his person should be out of danger, etc.'

In return, Charles suggested that he and Glenaladale should take an oath of fidelity to the men.

'That if danger should come upon them they would stand by one another to the last drop of their blood.'

However, the three men refused to accept this oath from Charles.

The next day saw the return of the other four Glen Moriston men. Once they had overcome the emotional reaction of meeting Charles, they took the same oath as their three friends. Whereupon, Charles remarked that they were all now the first privy council that had been sworn to him since the battle of Culloden. He promised that he would never forget them or theirs, if ever he came to his own.

This promise was received somewhat sceptically. One of the Glen Moriston men remarked that Charles' great-uncle, Charles II, had not been 'very mindful' of the friends who had helped in his restoration to the throne. Just as he had done at Corodale in reply to a similar comment from MacDonald of Boisdale, Charles apologised for his ancestor's neglect, and reassured the men that they might depend upon his own word as the word of a Prince.

The four men, who had just returned to Coire Dho, brought a dead deer and a live ox, which they slaughtered before the Prince. The Glen Moriston men had only recently finished drinking some bottles of wine that they had looted from the enemy. They were now 'angry with themselves for living so lordly upon the wine, as they might still have some of it for the Prince's use'.

The next few days, gave Charles the much needed opportunity to rest. On his arrival, he had been very unwell and 'troubled with a looseness'. After three days, he 'was so well refreshed that he thought himself able to encounter any hardships'. They then moved two miles away to take up residence in another cave, 'a grotto no less romantic than the former'.

Throughout this time, Charles joined wholeheartedly into the life of this community, and mixed easily with all the men. For reasons of security, the men did not address Charles by his royal title. He was given the alias, 'Dougal MacCullonoy', but everyone called him plain 'Dougal'.

He impressed the Glen Moriston men with the manner in which 'he bore up under all his misfortunes with great resolution and chearfulness, never murmuring or complaining at the hardships and severity of his condition'. Patrick Grant particularly noted that Charles used to say his prayers early every morning. 'I believe the Prince is a very good Christian indeed.'

As Charles could speak very little Erse, and the Glen Moriston men could speak no English, Glenaladale had to translate. In each other's company, the English-speakers and Erse-speakers said only that which they wanted to be communicated to the other.

Charles very quickly discovered that the Glen Moriston men were 'much addicted to common swearing'. Years later, Patrick Grant still remembered, 'at last the Prince by his repeated reproofs, prevailed on us so far that we gave that custom of swearing quite up'.

As Charles listened to the private conversations between the Erse-speakers, he was particularly intrigued by the frequent use of a phrase, which can be written phonetically as 'Hose Ian'. It was only some weeks later, that he learned that the phrase was actually 'Aos, Eain', meaning, 'Listen, John!', and was used to attract the attention of each of the three men called 'John MacDonald'!

Some of the men went out daily to observe the movement of troops, and obtain provisions. One day, these scouts reported that a company of militia was now camping just a few miles away. At this news, it was decided that Charles should move from the Glen Moriston area altogether. Leaving Alexander MacDonald and Alexander Chisholm to keep an eye on the militia, the others walked through the night to Strathglass.

Coire Mheadhoin from its head

Coire Dho

20
2 - 9 AUGUST
STRATHGLASS to
GLEN STRATHFARRAR

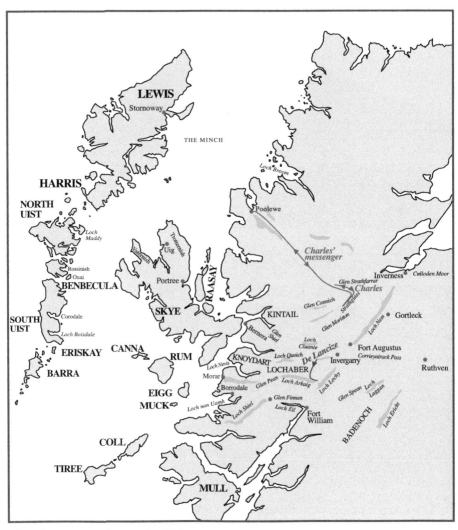

The various movements between 2 and 9 August

The Enemy

Albemarle continued to receive information from many different sources. Much of it was wild rumour.

'I am informed that He [Charles] may make his escape over the High Hills between Strathnaver and Sutherland into Cathness in two Days, and that the people of Cathness are great Rebels.'

(3 August, 1746)

'This moment (viz Aug 3d) I received Information from Allan McLean here the Pretender's Son, Lochiel and four more were in a Shield House in Glendeasrie Six days past, and on observing a party of the Military coming that way made their Escape to the Hill, and is Suspected to be return'd to the said Sheilling when the Party went off.'

(4 August, 1746)

Albemarle now ordered Campbell to march his men from the west coast to Glen Dessary, and meet up with Lord Loudoun's troops coming from the east.

The Friends

O'Sullivan Out in the North Sea, *Le Hardi Mendiant,* with the two privateers, was still battling against the storm, trying to reach the west coast of Scotland. Her two escorts now revealed themselves as only fair weather friends. They both abandoned *Le Hardi Mendiant* on 4 August, and returned to piracy.

Le Hardi Mendiant continued to tack, in the hope of making headway to the west. However, the ship now began to leak badly. With the departure of the privateers, she was desperately short of provisions. In the circumstances, there was no alternative but to abandon the attempt. Moreover, Dumont insisted that they should return to France, rather than Norway. Thus, on 8 August, the ship turned south.

De Lancize De Lancize and Berar had been taken into the safe protection of Donald MacDonnell of Loch Garry. The Frenchmen did not tell Lochgarry that they had really come to try and rescue Charles. They informed him only that they had letters to deliver to Charles. Although Lochgarry did not know where Charles was, he thought that Lochiel might know. He arranged for de Lancize and Berar to be taken to Loch Arkaig, where Dr Archibald Cameron would be able to put them in touch with Lochiel.

The Prince

The Prince's companions: Alexander MacDonald of Glen Aladale, John MacDonald (Glenaladale's brother), John MacDonald (Borrodale's son), Donald MacDonald, Patrick Grant, Gregor MacGregor, Alastair Chisholm, Donald Chisholm, Hugh Chisholm, John MacDonald and Alexander MacDonald.

In Strathglass, the Charles and his companions rested in some fir woods. Later, they went out in pairs to obtain information, and buy provisions. They returned with meal, butter, cheese, meat, whisky and tobacco, all bought from a man by the name of John Chisholm.

That evening, they were re-joined by Alexander MacDonald and Alexander Chisholm, who reported that the troops in Coire Dho were not a danger. It was decided that they should all spend the night where they were.

Two shiely huts were built out of branches. Charles shared one with Glenaladale and Young Borrodale. Charles was given the luxury of a bed made from a grass divot, some six or seven feet long.

The next day, Charles' thoughts turned once again to Poolewe. Instead of beginning the long trek there himself, he sent a scout to gather information. The next day, Charles' impatience got the better of him. That afternoon, he decided that they should move northwards in order to meet the scout returning. They walked five or six miles, spent the night in another shiely hut, and arrived in Glen Cannich about noon.

The next few days were spent in and around this glen. Most nights, they slept in shiely huts, but one night they were bold enough to stay in a village. One day, two of the party went back to John Chisholm to buy more provisions, while the rest waited on the crest of the ridge on the north side of Glen Cannich. According to local tradition, Charles went down from the ridge into Glen Strathfarrar, and stayed in a cave there.

One night, Charles and his friends celebrated the beginning of Lammas with a 'hearty drink'. Charles talked about his friends and family at home. In particular, he told them how he thought his own brother, Prince Henry, was 'preferable to himself in all respects, and as one of great spirits and activity'. He talked of the King of France as 'a true and fast friend', who would risk everything to save him. He felt very sure that the Dauphin also had a great regard for him.

As Charles relaxed, he told them of his love for one of the daughters of the King of France. She was 'a mighty fine agreeable lady, being sweet natured and humble', with hair 'as black as a raven'. They all drank her health, and, much to everybody's amusement, John MacDonald announced, 'As that lady is so good-natured, agreeable and humble, would to God we had her here, for we would take the best care of her in our power, and if possible be kinder to her than to your Royal Highness.'

Loch Carrie in Glen Cannich

154

'God forbid,' replied Charles, 'For were she here and seized, to ransom her person would make peace over all Europe upon any terms the Elector of Hanover would propose.'

They then all 'spoke upon this lady about a whole hour without intermission'.

'Had the daughter of France been with us we
would have made the best bed we could of
heather and ferns for the Prince and her,
and would kept sentry upon them that nobody
should have disturbed them.'

As they got to know him, Charles' friends began to notice some of his less appealing personal habits. They particularly disapproved of the fact that he 'did always sleep in his cloaths and plaid, in his wig and bonnet'. They were also disliked his practice of wearing the same shirt for about two weeks at a time. He changed it only when he was troubled with lice.

On 7 August, the scout returned from Poolewe to confirm that the French ship had left. However, the scout was also able to tell Charles of the French officers who had set off to find Charles in the land of the Camerons. Immediately, Charles decided that he must move to Loch Arkaig to try to meet these Frenchmen. During the night of 8 August, they all set off.

Glen Strathfarrar

21
9 - 15 AUGUST
STRATHGLASS to LOCH ARKAIG

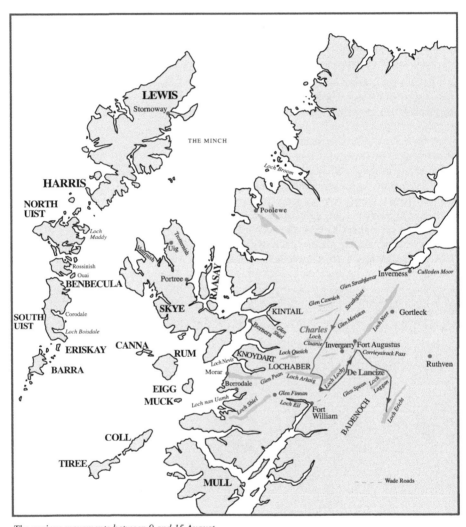

The various movements between 9 and 15 August

The Enemy

Albemarle was still receiving useless reports on Charles' whereabouts.

'... I arriv'd Yesterday morning by day break at Glendisary, but finding no party I search'd that whole country for five miles around, but could get no intelligence of the pretenders son having been there lately; there is but one Shiling in all Glendisary which is inhabited, we took two of these people after following them four miles; but after we had sworn them, and whip'd them severely with belts, they still declard that they had not heard of the pretenders son being there lately, but that Doctor Cameron had been there three days before.'

(10 August, 1746)

Albemarle continued to report this failure to Lord Newcastle.

'The last Party I sent out (upon a report that the Pretenders Son was in Glendassary) returned last night without any tidings of him, and I can make no conjecture of the place he lies concealed in, therefore cannot help suspecting he is gone off, either in some of the small French vessels that have been hovering along the coast, or in a Boat to the Long Island, for I am certain, the Report of his being in Badenoch was groundless, having had several Parties from the Dragoons quartered upon the Coast, and from the Foot at Aberdeen, Strathbogie, Castle Menzies and Blair, who have most narrowly searched that whole country.'

(12 August, 1746)

On 13 August, Albemarle decided to depart for Edinburgh with most of the troops. The small force left behind at Fort Augustus was put under the command of Lord Loudoun.

The Friends

The French The plans for the next mission were now finalised. Warren and O'Byrne would travel with 275 men in *L'Heureux*, while Lynch and Sheridan would have 225 men in *Le Prince de Conti*. The date for their departure was set for 19 August. So high was the state of secrecy, that Warren knew neither the date for departure, nor the fact that he would now have only two ships instead of the four originally planned.

Warren also did not know where in the whole of Scotland he should begin to look for Charles. The only information he had was that in O'Sullivan's vague coded letter, which had arrived several days before.

O'Sullivan As *Le Hardi Mendiant* approached the coast of Flanders, she had to run the gauntlet of the British ships blockading the French ports. Captain Dumont was able to evade interception by these ships, and reached Blankenburg on 13 August. O'Sullivan went ashore 'in full view of several enemy ships'. He immediately set off for Paris.

De Lancize At Loch Arkaig, de Lancize convinced Archibald Cameron that he and Berar were on a bona fide mission for the Prince's benefit. Archibald arranged to conduct the two Frenchmen to Lochiel, who was now in hiding twenty miles away in Badenoch. Before leaving, de Lancize decided to contact his companions on *Le Bien Trouvé*, which, he believed, was still cruising off Loch Broom. He sent two letters, using one of Lochiel's tenants, Euan MacVee, as messenger.

One letter, intended for Alexander MacLeod, was written in French so that it could be used to negotiate with Anguier or the commander of any other French ship that may have arrived at Loch Broom. The letter asked MacLeod to let de Lancize know if a French ship had appeared in Loch Broom. MacLeod was also to ask the commander to await the return of de Lancize. The other letter, written in English, was intended for a man they had met between Loch Broom and Loch Arkaig. He was requested to give the first letter to MacLeod or another Frenchman.

> 'Wee have been detained longer than we expected in this Countrey in pursuit of our bussiness and must continue ten days longer; if the Gentleman who brought us to the Country, who you saw, comes your way in search of us, desire him to continue going and comeing untill we go to the place apointed to meet him, and send the inclosed to him, att any rate desire him not to go off without us as he shall answer to his constituent; give him the inclosed, and if any other of our Countreymen come there before him, desire them to wait thereabout till we return, as we have bussiness of the outmost consequence upon hand: if you should be at any trouble or expence in sending to any of our friends that comes to your neighbourhood we shall pay you att meeting.'
>
> (13 August, 1746)

The Prince

The Prince's companions: Alexander MacDonald of Glen Aladale, John MacDonald (Glenaladale's brother), John MacDonald (Borrodale's son), Donald MacDonald, Patrick Grant, Gregor MacGregor, Alastair Chisholm, Donald Chisholm, Hugh Chisholm, Alexander Chisholm, John MacDonald and Alexander MacDonald.

Charles' companions knew that, in order to reach Loch Arkaig, it was necessary to cross Glen Moriston. If the soldiers, they had seen there a few days previously, were still about, it would be unwise to leave for Loch Arkaig immediately. Charles decided to send two scouts all the way to Lochiel's estate to reconnoitre. Meanwhile, he would wait in Strathglass, until the scouts returned.

None of the residents of Strathglass detected the presence of the fugitives in the forest. However, Charles' party was discovered accidentally by a lone traveller, Hugh MacMillan. Fortunately, he knew the Glen Moriston men very well, because he had fought in their regiment at Culloden. As he was a man they could trust, he was invited to join the Prince's service.

The fugitives continued to buy supplies from John Chisholm, who served them so generously that Charles wanted to meet him. Accordingly, Patrick Grant and Hugh Macmillan were sent to ask Chisholm 'to come along with them to see a friend whom he would like very well to see'. At this invitation, John sensed that some special event was in store.

'I believe there is some person of consequence amongst you, and as I have one bottle of wine (the property of a priest with whom I am in very great friendship), I will venture to take it along with me.'

'What, John!,' said Patrick Grant, 'Have you had a bottle of wine all this time and not given it to us before this time?'

Having served in the Prince's army, John Chisholm recognised Charles instantly. Patrick Grant presented Charles with the wine.

'I do not remember that your Royal Highness has drunken to me since you came among our hands.'

Before drinking from the bottle, Charles toasted the health of Patrick Grant and all his friends.

Now that John Chisholm realised the provisions he had sold to the Glen Moriston men had actually been for the Prince, he wanted to return every penny he had been paid. However, Charles insisted that John should keep the money. He asked only that John should take the same oath of loyalty and secrecy that had been taken by the Glen Moriston men.

On 11 August, the scouts returned with the news that the troops in Glen Moriston had left for Fort Augustus. It was now safe to cross the glen.

They set out at six o'clock next morning. Four hours later, they had reached the hills overlooking Glen Moriston, where they spent the rest of the day on a summit. At night, they set off again, but, after less than a mile, they learned that a strong detachment of soldiers had been sent to search for the Prince in the hills surrounding Glen Garry. As this was the next stage on their intended route, they decided to wait until the danger had gone. They found a shiely hut in which to spend the rest of the night.

The next day, they decided to send three scouts ahead. Two of them were to go all the way to Loch Arkaig, and inform Cameron of Clunes that Glenaladale wished to meet him. These two scouts were then to await the arrival of Charles on the shore of Loch Arkaig at Achnasaul. The third scout was to travel only as far as Glen Garry, and come back when the soldiers had left.

The waiting soon became too much for Charles. He announced that he wanted to move on without waiting for the scout to return. However, the Glen Moriston men refused to allow him to leave. They insisted that they knew what was safest for him, and told him of the great dangers they would face, if they left immediately. Soon the argument became so heated that the Glen Moriston men threatened to abandon Charles, if he would not follow their advice. They even threatened to tie him up, rather than comply with his demands.

Charles fell into a sulk, refusing to accept food and drink until his friends did what he wanted. The Glen Moriston men tried to cajole him with warnings that, without sustenance, he would not have strength for the journey ahead. Moreover, if they were attacked, he would not be able 'to act his part in any shape so well as he would wish to do'. They also assured Charles that, with their local knowledge, they could ensure that the enemy would not approach within two miles of them without being detected.

Finally, when Charles realised that the Glen Moriston men would not change their minds, he relented.

> 'I find kings and princes must be ruled by their privy council, but I believe there is not in all the world a more absolute privy council that what I have at present.'

Later, Patrick Grant and Alexander Chisholm went in search of provisions, and accidentally encountered the Laird of Glen Moriston. As the laird had been aware of their absence from the glen over the last few weeks, he enquired where and how they were now living. They replied 'that as the enemy were pillaging and plundering the country it were a pity not to share in the spoil, upon part of which they made a shift to live rather than that the enemy should have all'.

Unwittingly, the laird enquired whether they had any news of the Prince, and told them of rumours that Charles had passed the Braes of Knoydart. 'I wish,' he added, 'if he came this way that I might know of it, for he should be taken good care of.'

Although Patrick and Alexander knew the laird to be a trusty friend, they chose not to reveal their secret. Reporting back to Charles, they enquired whether the laird should be asked to help. Charles declined this offer. He was 'so pleased with his present guard, that he wanted none other, and that he had experienced poor folks to be as faithful as any men, rich or high, could be'.

On 14 August, the scout returned from Glen Garry with news that the way was now safe. As it was foggy, they decided to set off in the afternoon, rather than wait for darkness.

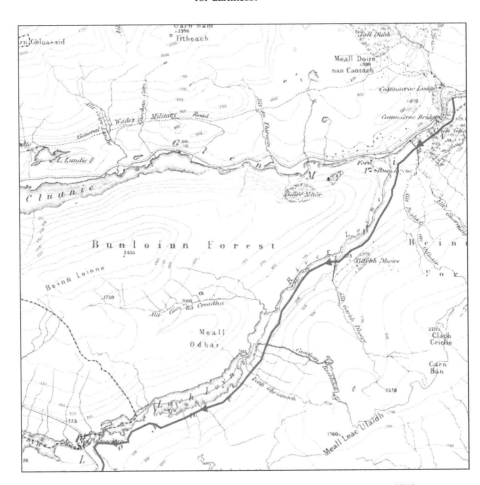

Charles' route through Glen Loyne, as it was in 1746

After these few days of rest, Charles was feeling much better. During the day, he walked so quickly that 'few persons could hold out with him'. However, he encountered difficulties during the night, because he was not used to such terrain in total darkness.

'... he was every now and then ... slumping into this and the other clayhole or puddle, insomuch that very often he would have been plashed up to the navel, having no breeches but a philabeg, and when he had arrived at any place to take a little rest, he would have taken a nook of his plaid and therewith have rubbed his belly and thighs to clean them the best way he could.'

Loch Loyne

After walking through Glen Loyne in heavy rain, they reached Glen Garry late at night. They found the river to be so swollen that they doubted it could be crossed. However, Charles 'positeivly insisted upon giving it a tryal' even though the night was very dark.

'Two of the company went first to try if they could wade the water, and found it passable, even though it came up to their very middle. Whereupon, his royal highness and the rest of his party entering the water, they forded it safely.'

Loch Garry

They walked on for another mile, and spent the
remainder of the night resting on the side of a hill
in the pouring rain. In the morning, they set off again,
with the rain still heavy. By ten o' clock, they had
crossed over the hills to Achnasaul.

The River Garry close to the crossing point

Loch Arkaig near Achnasaul

22

15 - 23 AUGUST
LOCH ARKAIG

Cameron of Lochiel

Dr Archibald Cameron

15 - 18 August

The Friends

The French Now that the preparations were complete, Warren was concerned to learn that his mission had been reduced from four ships to two.

'I little expected this Disappointment after all the delay already given, and having jaunted us up and down, I should have thought that they might give us the Sirene and the Dursley; however we must take patience, half-loaf is better that no Bread, and since we can't be our own carvers, we must be resigned. I trust in God I shall succeed in bringing back our Hero safe and sound as if I had ten frigatts, 'tis the height of my ambition, and I shall allways look upon it as the happiest action of my life, and I have great confidence that Providence has this Blessing in store for me.'

(18 August, 1746)

De Lancize and Lochiel The two Frenchmen met Lochiel in his bothy. There was an atmosphere of mutual suspicion. De Lancize still did not reveal his real purpose. He informed Lochiel only that Alexander MacLeod had important letters for Charles at Loch Broom.

Lochiel was not convinced that the Frenchmen were telling the truth. The fact, that they did not have the letters with them seemed suspicious. The excuse that the letters were at Loch Broom sounded far-fetched, particularly as the French men had had not mentioned this fact to Lochgarry.

Lochiel concluded that the Frenchmen might be government spies. However, he felt that every effort should be made to let Charles know about them. At the same time, Charles should be warned of the dubious circumstances.

Unfortunately, Lochiel did not know where Charles was. He had heard only rumours that Charles was on the mainland. Lochiel therefore decided that Archibald and Rev. John Cameron should try to find Charles. Initially, they were each to travel to Loch Arkaig by different routes, with Archibald taking the Frenchmen with him.

The Prince

The Prince's companions: Alexander MacDonald of Glen Aladale, John MacDonald (Glenaladale's brother), John MacDonald (Borrodale's son), Donald MacDonald, Patrick Grant, Gregor MacGregor, Alastair Chisholm, Alexander Chisholm, Donald Chisholm, Hugh Chisholm, John MacDonald, Alexander MacDonald and Hugh MacMillan.

With the rain pouring in torrents, Charles and his party sought somewhere to shelter at Achnasaul. However, all the cottages had been razed. They could find only a derelict shiely hut, 'a most inconvenient habitation, it raining as heavy within as without it'. To add to their misery, the fugitives were now very hungry. Apart from 'half a peck of meal' and some salt, they had used up their food hours ago.

Charles expected to meet the two friends they had sent from Glen Moriston. These scouts were expected to come to Achnasaul every morning until Charles arrived. As they had not done so on this particular day, Charles' patience had

reached its limits by the time the two men arrived in the late afternoon. They informed Charles that Cameron of Clunes could provide a hut in a nearby wood where they should all spend the night.

Patrick Grant and Alexander MacDonald were sent to inspect this place. By an amazing piece of good fortune, they found the hut occupied by a deer, which Patrick immediately shot. Charles was then informed that the shelter was safe, and given the good news about the menu for supper.

On learning that MacDonnell of Lochgarry was in hiding nearby, Charles decided to seek his help. While Glenaladale was dispatched to summon Lochgarry, the rest of the party went to the new hiding place, and spent the evening preparing the venison. Later, 'they were most deliciously feasted'. Lochgarry arrived in the evening.

> 'I came directly to where his Roy[ll] H[s]. was, and was overjoyed to kiss his hand. It gave me new courage to see his R. H[s]. safe, and really believed, once I had the happiness to meet H.R.H[s]., he would be afterwards safe in spite of his enemys.'

To everyone's great joy, Lochgarry told them all about the French officers Charles had come to meet.

The next morning, Clunes came with Cameron of Achnasaul. In the afternoon, Clunes led Charles and the others to a better hiding place in a wood at the east end of Loch Arkaig. Here, they were able to set up a more substantial base.

On being informed of the recent arrival of the Frenchmen, Charles decided not to follow them to Badenoch. He planned instead to make contact with a message via Lochiel. Clunes sent one of Lochiel's tenants, John Macpherson, to go to

Badenoch, and inform Lochiel where Charles now was. Meanwhile, Lochgarry placed twenty Kennedys as look-outs on the road from Fort Augustus to Loch Arkaig.

During the next few days, Lochgarry tried to persuade Charles to restart the hostilities, using the money that had been unloaded from *Le Mars* and *La Bellone*.

> '... I told him that there was still a considerable party wou'd rise in arms...., and I believed he wou'd very soon make a flying army of about two thousand men, and that the people were so terribly exasperated against Cumberland for his cruel behaviour that one of them wou'd be worth two before the battle and wou'd be much the safest way for his R.H^s. person, and as there was now plenty of money, his army wou'd turn very numerous, especially as the affection generally of the whole kingdom was now for him.'

Charles was interested in the idea, and replied that he would discuss the possibility with Lochiel and Cluny. However, Lochgarry was impatient and ready for more immediate action.

> '... I engaged Glengarie's people shou'd be ready in eight and forty hours, and obliged myself that with them I shoud attack and surprize Fort Augustus, and destroy or apprehend all the enemy there, being at that time about 800 men twixt regular and militia.'

Charles was not willing to be so precipitate. Eventually, he was able to restrain Lochgarry.

One day, a troop of soldiers drove some cattle along Loch Arkaig. According to tradition, Charles avoided discovery by hiding inside the trunk of a hollow tree. Later that day, Charles' friends were contemplating travelling sixteen miles to buy some food. However, Charles thought that none of the men was fit enough to make such a journey. Also, it was not certain that food would be available at the destination. Instead, he suggested that they should raid the herd that had just passed through.

'What would ye think, gentlemen,' said he, 'of lifting some of the cattle we spied under a command this evening? They are not far from us, and I hope we will succeed in the design, for the gloom of the night will favour us in the attempt.'

At first, his companions considered the idea to be too risky, but he eventually persuaded them.

'If the dangers attending this expedition be all that can be said against it, I myself will be one of the number that will make the attempt.'

Four of his friends volunteered to join him, and 'by the favour of the dark night they brought off six cows without being in the least discovered'.

The next day, one of the cows was slaughtered. Charles supervised roasting it on a spit. He now knew the servants well by name, and gave them friendly directions in Erse 'about the homely cookery '.

18 - 23 August

The Friends

O'Sullivan O'Sullivan reached Paris on 18 August. He immediately began agitating with Louis and the French ministers to mount another rescue attempt. With the support of Charles' brother, O'Sullivan finally persuaded the French to provide three small ships, including

Le Hardi Mendiant, for an expedition to be led by O'Sullivan himself.

Warren The very day that O'Sullivan arrived in Paris, Warren and the other three Irishmen assembled in Brittany, some 200 miles away. In the two days before they set off, it is possible that O'Sullivan managed to contact Warren, and advise him where was the best place to make contact with Charles. While, there is no evidence that such a message was ever sent, it is interesting that, when Warren set sail on 20 August, he was intent on landing at Loch Boisdale in South Uist - exactly where O'Sullivan would have advised him to go first. However, it is also the place

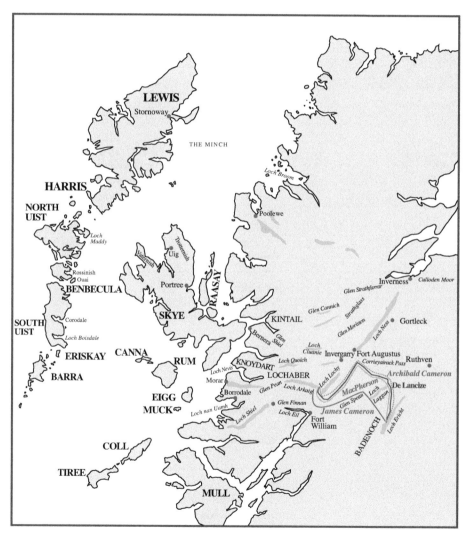

The various movements between 18 and 23 August

The River Arkaig at Achnacarry

where Warren's companion, Lynch, who had recently returned from Scotland, would have recommended that they should start the search.

Archibald Cameron and de Lancize After travelling only a few miles from Lochiel's hiding place, Archibald Cameron and the two Frenchmen met John MacPherson taking his message to Lochiel. MacPherson refused to divulge anything to Archibald Cameron. He revealed only that he had 'business of the utmost consequence', which he could give only to Lochiel personally. Suspecting that the message could affect the usefulness of his own mission, Archibald decided that they should all return to his brother with MacPherson.

At the news of Charles' arrival at Loch Arkaig, Lochiel arranged for the Frenchmen to lodge with some of his friends. Meanwhile, Archibald was to travel with four servants to meet Charles.

At Achnacarry, Archibald met Rev. John Cameron who had been 'travelling and searching several days to no purpose'. John was amazed to be told that Charles was just a few hundred yards across the river. As the water in the river was too high to wade, they raised a submerged boat that had been skuttled by enemy troops. Just as they were about to cross, they caught sight of two armed men on the far bank. However, Clunes' children, told them that the armed men were actually guards provided by their father. Archibald and John then announced that they intended to hide in the wood for some days. They dismissed the servants on the pretext that it would be too dangerous to hide everyone there.

The Prince

The Prince's companions: Alexander MacDonald of Glen Aladale, John MacDonald (Glenaladale's brother), John MacDonald (Borrodale's son), Donald MacDonald, Patrick Grant, Gregor MacGregor, Alastair Chisholm, Donald Chisholm, Hugh Chisholm, Alexander Chisholm, John MacDonald, Alexander MacDonald and Hugh MacMillan.

Charles met Archibald and John in a hut. Charles was 'bare-footed, had an old black kilt coat on, a plaid, philabeg and waistcoat, a dirty shirt and a long red beard, a gun in his hand, a pistol and durk by his side. He was very cheerful and in good health, and, in my opinion fatter than when he was at Inverness'.

Charles was delighted to see his visitors. Archibald apologised for Lochiel being unable to come, and explained that his brother's wounds still made it very difficult for him to travel far. On hearing that Lochiel was actually well and recovering, Charles 'thanked God thrice for it'. Charles invited his new guests to a meal of roast beef - more spoils of the previous day's raid on the herd of cattle. Archibald contributed some bread he had bought in Fort Augustus on the way to Loch Arkaig.

'The Prince had a good appetite and we all sate in a circle when eating and drinking, every one having his morsel on his own knee, and the Prince would never allow us to keep off our bonnets when in his company.'

After listening to the story about the Frenchmen, Charles shared Lochiel's suspicions. 'He said it was surprizing that two men, strangers, and without one word of Earse, could escape from the troops.'

Nevertheless, he still wanted to meet them, and and arranged their recall from Badenoch. He also made a plan to avoid any harm they might do to him when they were face-to-face.

Charles wrote them a letter, explaining that he was now hiding in a very remote area, and, instead of coming to meet them himself, he was sending 'Captain Drummond' to receive their message. Charles planned to assume the identity of 'Captain Drummond', and interview the Frenchmen.

Although de Lancize had been on *Elisabeth*, the ship that had set out to accompany Charles on the journey from France the previous year, he had never actually seen Charles. Thus, both Frenchmen did not recognise Charles, or suspect who 'Captain Drummond' really was. During their stay of two or three days, they told 'Captain Drummond' everything they wanted to communicate to Charles. Unfortunately, this was all 'of no great consequence'. When Charles was satisfied that the Frenchmen were of no use, they were conducted away.

Hoping that the letters left with Alexander MacLeod may be more informative, Charles sent a messenger to Loch Broom for them. However, the letters that were sent were all in code directed to the French ambassador. Charles could make nothing of them.

It seems likely that Charles was able to inform the Frenchmen of the fate of their ship, *Le Bien Trouvé*. If he had not done so, de Lancize and Berar, would have made their way back to meet their ship. De Lancize probably told Charles about other impending rescue attempts, because Charles immediately ordered Glenaladale's brother and Young Borrodale to return to their homes at the coast. There, they were to keep watch on all the shipping, and keep Charles informed of any French ships that arrived.

Charles decided that he wanted to wait for these ships in Badenoch with Lochiel and Cluny. However, his friends advised him that it was too risky for him to travel there immediately. The newspapers were currently reporting that he had only recently crossed the Corrieyairack pass with Lochiel and a band of thirty men. If the troops also believed this story, they certainly would be searching the route to Badenoch.

Charles therefore agreed to remain at Loch Arkaig until this danger had passed. Nevertheless, he sent Archibald and Lochgarry to inform Lochiel and Cluny of his wish to join them, and to ask for their advice as to whether he should revive the rebellion.

23
23 - 28 AUGUST
LOCH ARKAIG to GLEN KINGIE

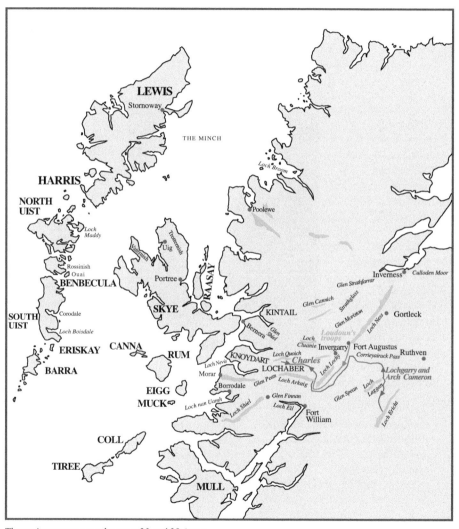

The various movements between 23 and 28 Augus

The Enemy

Albemarle From the comfort and civilisation of Edinburgh, Albemarle wrote to Lord Loudoun in Fort Augustus.

> 'I suppose as your Lordship was at Inverness the 21st, the time appointed to put those orders in execution I left with you against Mr Barrisdale and his country, is the reason I have not heard of your success in that affair.'
>
> (27 August, 1746)

He also informed Loudoun of the Duke of Newcastle's order that the forces at Fort Augustus must be reduced immediately to only those in Loudoun's own regiment.

Loudoun Albemarle's reminder was unnecessary, because Loudoun had already sent a force to arrest Barrisdale. Loudoun, himself, had gone to Inverness in response to a request from Major-General Blakeney. This request followed a letter from Lord Fortrose.

Lord Loudoun

> 'One of My Tenents in Kintail brought me here a Rebell Express Prisoner, with the two inclosed Letters that the fellow had carefully concealed.
> I thought proper to send both him and his Packet directly to you, as he is a Rebell and wont confess whence he came or where he was going. If I am not mistaken the Person that signs the Letters is one

the five that landed in Lochbroom, and was intrusted with Letters to the young Pretender. '

(25 August, 1746)

The prisoner was Euan MacVee, the messenger de Lancize had sent with letters for Alexander MacLeod at Loch Broom. At Inverness, MacVee 'got five hunderd lashes, being ty'd to a stake and beaten. Some days after he got five hundred more, and they threaten'd to whip him to death if he did not discover what they wanted.'

However, he divulged nothing. As he lay bleeding in prison, he refused to eat the meal thrown to him by the soldiers. Other prisoners urged him to save himself by telling what he knew. They derided him as a fool, but he maintained his proud defiance.

> 'You are the fool. It signifies nothing what they can do to me (Let them do the worst) in respect of what could be done to those from whom I had and to whom I was going with the letters. Their deaths will be great loss, but mine will be none.'

Sadly, MacVee was to die in prison within a few days.

MacVee's arrest was reported to Albemarle by Loudoun in a callous, casual manner.

> 'I came hear late last night, being sent for by M.G. Blakeney on some letters [that] had been intersepted in Kintail from Mos. La Luize of no great importance.'
>
> (27 August, 1746)

Barrisdale At his home, the traitor was well aware that he had not delivered the goods, and that his time was now up. This fact was common knowledge among all the government troops. At Bernera barracks, one Captain Powell took it upon himself to raid the traitor's home, and seize cattle for himself. Somehow, Barrisdale was warned before Powell's troops arrived on 23 August. He was able to escape in a boat with his son.

The Friends

While O'Sullivan tried to organise another rescue mission from France, *L'Heureux* and *Le Prince de Conti* sailed steadily northwards. A few days after setting sail, they were chased by a hostile ship, but managed to give it the slip under the cover of darkness. In Scotland, the mission of de Lancize was finished. He and Berar languished in safety with the Camerons.

The Prince

The Prince's companions: Alexander MacDonald of Glen Aladale, Donald MacDonald, Patrick Grant, Gregor MacGregor, Alastair Chisholm, Hugh Chisholm, Donald Chisholm, Hugh Chisholm, John MacDonald, Alexander MacDonald, Hugh MacMillan, Rev. John Cameron.

Early in the morning of 23 August, John Cameron and Clunes left their hideout in the woods, and visited Clunes' family, now living in a hut. After half an hour, a young girl came rushing to inform them that a large force of troops was approaching. While Clunes remained in hiding to observe these soldiers, his son, and John Cameron went to inform Charles. By the time they were within a pistol shot of Charles' hut, John could see the troops approaching fast. On being woken to this dire news, Charles' calmly called for his guns, and summoned his sentries. By the time Clunes arrived, Charles had eight men about him. However, they were hopelessly outnumbered'.

> '... we were determined, rather than to yield, to be butchered by our merciless enemies to sell our lives dear and in defence of our Prince to die like men of honour.'

They left the hut, and climbed unseen through the trees to the top of a hill above the wood. Here, they waited for the enemy to follow.

> 'The Prince examined all our guns, which were in pretty good order, and said he hoped we would do some execution before we were killed. For his part he was bred a fowler, and could charge quick, was a tolerable marksman, and would be sure of one at least.'

The enemy did not follow. Even when they found the hut in which Charles had met the Frenchmen, they did not realise that Charles had been there. The soldiers left, taking ten milk cows that Clunes had recently bought.

Eventually, Charles sent Clunes and John Cameron down the hill to reconnoitre. While he waited for them to return, Charles moved further up Gleann Cia-aig to the top of Meall an Tagraidh. He then sent Clunes' son to inform Clunes where he had gone. Round about midnight, all three men returned to report to Charles. They were able to tell Charles that these soldiers were actually on their way to arrest Barrisdale under the orders of Lord Loudoun. It was a great relief to

Charles that they had not arrived as a result of someone betraying him. Nevertheless, Charles was disappointed that Lochgarry's look-outs had not been able to give a warning of the approaching troops.

It was obviously unsafe to return to the valley immediately. Charles and his friends spent the rest of the night on the mountain. They had bread and cheese together with 'a hearty dram', which Clunes had brought from the valley. For warmth, they risked lighting a fire for half an hour.

Since they considered it too dangerous to travel in daylight, they decided to stay where they were for the whole of the following day. Despite the cold and several hailstorms, Charles, covered by his plaid, was able to sleep all morning.

As it was still too risky to return to Loch Arkaig, they descended Meall Coire nan Saobadh to the remote Glen Kingie. There, they 'lived merrily for several days', and had the good fortune to find a cow which they killed for meat. When they eventually retraced their steps to Loch Arkaig, they did not go back to their old huts in the valley. For safety, they remained in the hills overlooking the loch. Charles 'lay that night and the next day in open air, and though his cloaths were wet he did not suffer the least in health'.

While waiting for Lochgarry and Archibald Cameron to return, Charles decided that he no longer needed the services of the Glen Moriston men.

Before dismissing them, he told them that he intended to pay them for all their help, when Lochgarry and Archibald Cameron returned with some money from Lochiel. He asked Patrick Grant to stay behind to receive this payment. As the others took their leave, Charles promised, 'If ever in his power he would make satisfaction for there losses and gratitue.'

A few days later, Charles decided that, with the impending move to Badenoch, Glenaladale would now serve him better by going home so that he could watch for

Meall Coire nan Saobhadh

Meall an Tagraidh

French ships at the coast. It was arranged that, if one arrived, Glenaladale would inform Clunes, who would know where Charles could be found.

On 27 August, Lochgarry and Archibald Cameron returned from their errand to Badenoch. Charles was delighted to learn that Lochiel and Cluny wanted him to join them in Badenoch, and that Cluny would come in two days' time to take Charles there. Archibald and Lochgarry also told Charles that both Lochiel and Cluny were against the suggestion of restarting hostilities.

> '... in their opinion, as the kingdom was so full of the enemy, it wou'd be of much worse consequence to rise in arms than doe otherwise.'

Charles was now so impatient to leave, that he would not wait for Cluny to arrive. Hoping to encounter Cluny on the way, he set off the very next morning in the company of Lochgarry, Archibald Cameron and John Cameron, together with Clunes' son, Sandy, and three servants. Patrick Grant walked with them as far as the River Lochy, where Charles gave him 24 guineas to be shared among all the Glen Moriston men.

Patrick Grant's departure marked the end of a team, that had served the Prince with amazing dedication and loyalty. All the men and their families had undergone great personal sacrifice.

> '... so secret and cautious they were in their office that they never went near their wives and familys from the minute they met their Prince, and their poor wives concluded they were either kill'd, or taken by the enemy.'

When Young Borrodale and Glenaladale's brother returned home, 'they found their families to be in greatest distress for want of all necessarys of life, or houses to shelter us from the inclemency of the weather'.

At times, all the men had to endure the extremes of physical adversity. Without any cover, they had withstood whole days and nights of rain, wind and cold. They had experienced long periods of hunger, while having to summon sufficient strength and stamina to tackle many miles of the most rugged and inhospitable terrain. To deal with only these problems would have demanded exceptional courage. However, there was also the constant danger of a determined enemy. The men knew perfectly well that there would have been no mercy if they had been captured by the troops.

The motivating force giving rise to all these qualities was simple loyalty. It was also a mature loyalty that could endure Charles' petty, truculent tantrums such as that which he threw in the braes of Glen Moriston. 'This was the only time, said Patrick Grant, that we ever differed with the Prince in any one thing, and we were very sorry for it.'

This loyalty did not stop when these men left Charles. The Glen Moriston men made and kept yet another vow - that they would tell nobody about their adventures with the Prince until a year and a day had elapsed from the time they left Charles' service.

Finally, with so many men in Charles' retinue, it is remarkable that not one yielded to the temptation of the reward offered by the Hanoverians.

> 'They knew well the reward declar'd to give for apprehending or destroying H.R.Hˢ., but all the bribes in the world cou'd not make them betray that trust.'

24
28 - 29 AUGUST
LOCH ARKAIG to GLEN SPEAN

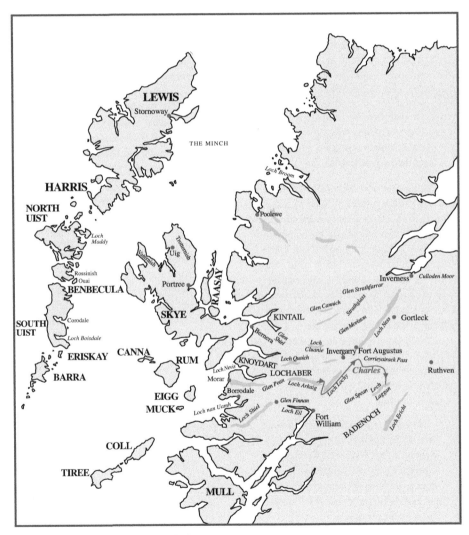

The various movements between 28 and 29 August

The Prince

The Prince's companions:
Donald MacDonnell of Loch Garry,
Dr Archibald Cameron,
Rev John Cameron, Alexander Cameron
(Clune's son)

The whole journey was planned very carefully by Lochgarry. He used his own men as advance- and rear-guards.

> 'I then gott together my trusty and brave party of fifty men, of your people, devideing them in two's and three's sent them to different arts for fear of being surpriz'd on our march by the enemy, they being spread over the whole country.'

Charles' guides were aiming to enter Badenoch at Loch Laggan in Glen Spean. The most direct route from Loch Arkaig is round the south end of Loch Lochy, south-west down the Great Glen, and then east along Glen Spean. However, from the very meagre information written about Charles' route to Loch Laggan, it is clear that he did not go this way.

> 'We were oblidg'd to pass within two short miles of Fort Augustus, where the body of the enemy lay encamped, but were in no danger of a surprize, by the vigilance of our little detatchment.'

Thus, Charles must have gone north-east up the Great Glen, and turned south-east to climb by Glen Tarff over the Corrieyairack Pass. Instead of the direct route of some twenty miles along Glen Spean, Charles' guides preferred one more than twice as long. Moreover, it is clear that this detour was preferred by Charles' friends in earlier journey's between Loch Arkaig and Badenoch. For example, Archibald Cameron had passed through Fort Augustus a week or so previously in returning to Loch Arkaig from Lochiel's hideout.

Unfortunately, Lochgarry gives no explanation for this chosen route. It is possible that the reason is connected with the fact that the area at the entrance to Glen Spean, was a very large drovers' stance. Here, the cattle, destined for the south, stopped overnight before continuing along Glen Spean, or down the Great Glen. Moreover, all the cattle, that the troops had confiscated, would have collected there. Such a large herd would have required many soldiers to guard it. Glen Spean was therefore a place to be avoided by Charles and his companions.

According to tradition, Charles' party reached Loch Laggan after walking over the shoulder of Creag Meagaidh, and down Coire Arder. At Aberarder House, Charles met Alexander MacDonnell of Tullochcrom, and his brother, Ranald. Although both brothers had been captains in Charles' army at Culloden, they had recently been able to make peace with Lord Loudoun. Officially, they were now helping the troops to search for the Prince. However, Alexander gave Charles a brown short coat, a shirt and a pair of shoes. In recounting his adventures, Charles told Alexander that 'he had learned now to know the 4th part of peck of meal, upon which he had once lived for about eight days'.

Despite his hopes, Charles did not meet Cluny Macpherson on the way. Cluny had travelled to Loch Arkaig by a different route. As a consequence, he arrived at Achnacarry to discover that Charles had already left. Frustrating as it was, there was no alternative for Cluny but to retrace his steps to meet Charles in Badenoch.

The remains of Wade's road by Loch Loch Lochy

Upper Glen Tarff

The head of Coire Arder

25
29 AUGUST - 6 SEPTEMBER
GLEN SPEAN to LOCH ERICHT

The various movemements between 29 August and 6 September

The Enemy

The achievements of Lord Albemarle in suppressing the rebellion had been much appreciated in London. Lord Newcastle had recently written to him expressing the king's satisfaction, and confirming Albemarle's appointment as Commander-in-Chief in Scotland.

In his reply, Albemarle could only report no improvement in his intelligence.

'You need not have recommended to me the preventing the Pretender's Son's escape, or the apprehending him if possible, for, to do the last, I should with infinite Pleasure walk bare foot from Pole to Pole, but we have no sort of inteligence about him, which makes me imagine that he is either gone to the Long Island, or that he died of misery in some of his hidden Places, Capt O'Neille, the French Officer, having told me that when he parted from him he was covered with a scorbutic humour, and one McLeod, taken since, declared that at the time he was seized he had the Bloody flux; this is all I have known for some time, intelligence being very difficult to obtain, notwithstanding my promises of reward and recommendation to Mercy.'

(1 September, 1746)

The Friends

After an uneventful voyage round the west coast of Ireland, *L'Heureux* and *Le Prince de Conti* arrived at South Uist on 4 September. Over the next two days, several expeditions were sent ashore to obtain information. Eventually, they encountered Neil MacEachain, who informed them that Charles was now on the mainland. With MacEachain as their pilot, they set sail for Loch nan Uamh on 6 September.

At this same time, an informer based on Skye was sending news of their arrival to Lord Loudoun.

'Yesterday Two French Vessels, one Forty and ther other of thirty Guns, came to Anchor at the Entry of Loch Boisdale; they landed Fifty men and marched to Kilbride, being three miles from the place they came on shore; they gave out they were English and demanded fresh provisions; after asking several questions and hearing that the Independant Companies in the Island were assembling to attack them, they marched to Reimbark, taking with them one Rory McDonald and three men of the Country, whom they carried on board with them and made them drunk in hopes to get some intelligence from them about the Pretender's Son and some of the principall Rebel Officers, which they not being able to   do either by threats or fair promises, they put put Rory McDonald and one of the Country men on shore, and carried off the other two who were willing to stay with them; the said McDonald says they were to go through the Inner Sounds of Skye, and that they durst not go home without carrying off the Pretender's Son or losing their ships.'

(6 September, 1746)

The Prince

The Prince's companions: Donald MacDonnell of Loch Garry, Dr Archibald Cameron, Rev. John Cameron, Alexander Cameron (Clunes' son).

After the brief stop at Aberarder, Charles and his friends were anxious to press on to Lochiel's hideout. Late at night, they reached Coire an Iubhair Mor. Even though they were now only two miles away from their destination, they decided to spend the night where they were. The next morning, they walked to Lochiel's bothy at Meallan Odhar, on the other side of the ridge.

This total journey from Loch Arkaig, a distance of about 55 miles, had been completed in just over 24 hours. They had done it 'without much eating or any sleep, but slumbering now and then on a hillside'.

'Our indefatigable Prince bore this with greater courage and resolution than any of us, nor never was there a Highlander born cou'd travel up and down hills better or suffer more fatigue. Show me a king or prince in Europe cou'd have born the like, or a tenth part of it.'

Lochiel was in the bothy with Young Breakachie. They were attended by Lochiel's principal servant, Allan Cameron, together with two of Cluny's servants. Lochiel spotted Charles and his party, while they were some distance away, but he did not recognise them immediately. Seeing that they were armed, he feared that they were soldiers or armed militia on patrol.

Coire an Iubhair Mor

183

As he was too lame to run away, Lochiel decided to make a fight of it, if the newcomers should turn out to be hostile. Lochiel was confident of winning, because he and his friends had more and better weapons. They also had the advantage of surprise and good cover.

Fortunately, Lochiel did not give the order to fire, before he recognised Charles and the others. Joyfully, Lochiel hobbled out of the bothy to greet Charles. As he tried to kneel in obeisance, Charles restrained him.

'Oh no, my dear Lochiel!' exclaimed Charles, clapping him on the shoulder. 'You don't know who may be looking from the tops of yonder hills, and if they see any such motions they'll immediately conclude that I am here, which may prove of bad consequence.'

Although the bothy was very primitive and 'of a very narrow compass', Young Breakachie had ensured that it was very well supplied with provisions.

'There was plenty of mutton newly killed, and an anker of whiskie of twenty Scotch pints, with some good beef sassers made the year before, and plenty of butter and cheese, and besides, a large well cured bacon ham.'

On entering the bothy, Charles 'took a hearty dram' with 'some minch'd collops dress'd with butter'.

'Now, gentlemen, I live like a Prince,' he said, as he ate the collops out of a saucepan with a silver spoon.

Thereafter, Charles 'was gay, hearty, and in better spirits than it was possible to think he could be, considering the many disasters, misfortunes, disappointments, fatigues, and difficulties he had undergone'. Frequently, he would call for a dram to drink the health of his friends.

Two days later, Cluny arrived from his futile journey to Achnacarry. As he made to kneel, Charles checked him, and kissed

Ben Alder

him as an equal. Charles' first words were intended to comfort Cluny, who felt guilty about not being at Culloden in time for the battle.

'I'm sorry, Cluny, you and your regiment were not at Culloden. I did not hear till of very late that you was so near to have come up with us that day.'

Cluny now took charge. He arranged for Charles to have new shirts made very quickly by his three sisters, who lived at Breakachie. He also decided that all the fugitives should move further into Ben Alder. The next day, they walked two miles to Uisge Chaoil Reidhe to stay in a bothy, which was 'superlatively bad and smockie'.

'Yet his Royal Highness took with everything.'

Although they expected a rescue ship to come to the west coast, Cluny decided that they should also investigate the possibility of Charles escaping from the east. He therefore ordered Young Breakachie to find John Roy Stewart, and go with him to try and hire a ship there.

Two or three days later, Cluny took Charles and the others to Leitir nan Leac above Loch Ericht. Here, Cluny had arranged the construction of 'a very romantic comical habitation'.

Loch Ericht

185

'It was really a curiosity, and can scarcely be described to perfection. Twas situate in the face of a very rough high rockie mountain called Letternilichk, which is still a part of Benalder, full of great stones and crevices and some scattered wood interspersed. The habitation called the *Cage* in the face of that mountain was within a small thick bush of wood. There was first some rows of trees laid down in order to level a floor for the habitation, and as the place was steep this rais'd the lower side to equall height with the other; and these trees, in the way of jests or planks, were entirely well levelled with earth and gravel. There were betwixt the trees, growing naturally on their own roots, some stakes fixed in the earth, which with the trees were interwoven with ropes made of heath and birch twigs all to the top of the Cage, it being of a round or rather oval shape, and the whole thatched and covered with foge. This whole fabrick hung as it were by a large tree, which reclined from one all along the roof to the other, and which gave it the name of the Cage; and by chance there happen'd to be two stones at a small distance from other in the side next the precipice resembling the pillars of a bosom chimney, and here was the fire placed. The smock had its vent out there, all along a very stonny plat of the rock, which and the smock were all together so much of a colour that any one coud make no difference in the clearest day, the smock and stones by and through which it pass'd being of such true and real resemblance. The Cage was no larger than to contain six or seven persons, four of which number were frequently employed in playing at cards, one idle looking on, one becking and another firing bread and cooking.'

The traditional site of Cluny's Cage

'The uper room served for *salle a manger* and bed chamber while the lower serv'd for a cave to contain liquors and other necessaries, at the back part was a proper hearth for cook and baiker, and the face of the mountain had so much the colour and resemblance of smock, no person cou'd ever discover that there was either fire or habitation in the place. Round this lodge were placed their sentinels at proper stations, some nearer and some at greater distances, who dayly brought them notice of what happened in the country, and even in the enemie's camps, bringing them likewise the necessary provisions, while a neighbouring fountain supplied the society with the rural refreshment of pure water.'

26

6 - 14 SEPTEMBER
LOCH ERICHT to GLEN SPEAN

The various movements between 6 and 12 September

6 - 12 September

The Enemy

Albemarle's intelligence reports were still wide of the mark.

'... the young Pretender and Lochiele were skulking about the Braes of Locharkaig and Auchnacarry.'

'... the young pretender just now is hid underneath ground in a sort of Cave in the Isle of Mull near the house of Jerlvick McLean, whose youngest son it seems is with him.'

'Col° John Roy Stewart having been sent by the Pretender after his overthrow at Culloden to France with Tydings, he returned a fourthnight ago, and landed at Lochbroom or Pulue, with upwards of £20,000 in gold, and a dozen Officers - I have not heard the number of private men, but certain it is that Lochiel and his prince are still in Lochaber.'

Albemarle preferred yet another version, which he communicated to Lord Newcastle.

'[I] have heard from the North for certain that the Pretender's son sailed in a small French Cutter from the Western Coast in Kintaill in the night of the 19th of last month.'

(9 September, 1746)

At the coast, General Campbell had long lost Charles' scent, and, despite being certain that Charles was still in Scotland, he was beginning to be discouraged.

'... my spirits begin to flag so I must conclude by beging you to let me know if whilst I stay here I can be of any use to the publick or to the Earle.'

(8 September, 1746)

The Friends

Round about four o'clock in the afternoon, *L'Heureux* and *Le Prince de Conti* entered Loch nan Uamh, where a little English meal ship, *May,* was taking shelter from a gale. Since the newcomers were sailing under English colours, the crew of *May* welcomed aboard a party of men from the French ships. Only when their guests arrested them in the name of the King of France, did they realise the awful truth. The *May* was then put under the command of a French officer and six men.

The local inhabitants around the loch were naturally apprehensive about the arrival of two ships in English colours. In particular, Borrodale went to hide in the hills with his family. He deputed a visiting tailor, Donald MacDonald, to discover the purpose of the ships.

In the evening, Captain O'Byrne came ashore, with Sir Thomas Sheridan's nephew, Michael. They asked to meet various local inhabitants by name. They also indicated that the purpose of their visit was to rescue the Prince. When Donald MacDonald conveyed this message to Borrodale, he brought his family out of hiding to meet the visitors. Sheridan had spent some time with the Borrodales in May, before leaving with *Le Mars* and *La Bellone*. He was therefore well-known to them, and, after much cautious questioning, he was able to convince them of his intention. Eventually, they assured him that they could help.

The next day, one of Borrodale's sons took Sheridan and O'Byrne to

Glenaladale, who, according to plan, set off to inform Cameron of Clunes at Loch Arkaig. Glenaladale was disappointed to find that Clunes had left the area, without leaving any instructions or messages. By pure accident, he met a woman who was able to tell him where Clunes was. Finally, Glenaladale found Clunes in a shieling.

The only person familiar with the route to Badenoch was John MacPherson, who, some weeks earlier, had carried Charles' message to inform Lochiel of Charles' arrival at Loch Arkaig. While Glenaladale returned to Loch nan Uamh, John was now commissioned to inform Charles of the arrival of the ships.

The Prince

The Prince's companions:
Donald MacDonnell of Loch Garry,
Dr Archibald Cameron, Rev. John
Cameron, Donald Cameron of Lochiel,
Ewan MacPherson of Cluny.

Oblivious of these happenings, Charles was enjoying life at Cluny's Cage.

'He sat and drank all the time pretty well and hearty, and seem'd to be quite reconcil'd with his entertainment.'

It was generally agreed that there was no hope of reviving the rebellion. Also, there was no point in any of the present residents of Cluny's Cage trying to live the rest of their lives in Scotland. Inevitably, they would all eventually be caught and executed. The only future for them was to escape to France with Charles.

It was decided to make yet another attempt to find a ship. Rev. John Cameron was commissioned to travel to Edinburgh to make the arrangements.

Meanwhile, there had to be contingency arrangements if a ship could not be found. They began constructing some winter quarters.

'In this house they contrived a particular room for the Prince which was to be floored with boards, lined with boards and covered within the roof with the same.'

Charles also wanted to make arrangements in preparation for a return with French troops. In particular, he wanted to ensure that the gold buried in Gleann Camgharaidh was well looked after. This responsibility was assigned to Cluny, who, with Young Breakachie, was to remain behind, rather than escape to France with the others. Only Dr Archibald Cameron knew exactly where the gold was hidden. It was therefore essential that he should take Cluny to learn this secret.

12 - 14 September,

The Friends
Dr Archibald Cameron and Cluny
In the pitch-black night of 12 September, Archibald and Cluny set off with two servants to Loch Arkaig. Just as Archibald's previous journey from Badenoch to Loch Arkaig had been blessed with a chance meeting with John MacPherson, he now miraculously encountered the same man again with another vital message. Had John arrived at the bothy on Meallan Odhar, where he expected Charles to be, he would have found nobody there. There would also have been no message to direct him to Cluny's Cage.

'And this chance meeting was certainly a very great providence,

*The various movements between
12 and 14 September*

since if it had happened otherwise the Prince would not have known the shipping's arrival till the return from Locharchaik.'

On hearing John MacPherson's news, Archibald directed one of his servants to take John to Charles. Cluny sent a message to Young Breakachie, advising him and John Roy Stewart to return to Charles immediately. Then, Archibald and Cluny continued their journey to Loch Arkaig.

Young Breakachie The message from Cluny arrived just as Young Breakachie was about to go to bed. His wife, heavily pregnant, complained bitterly about her husband leaving her and their many children in such a 'dismal situation'. Young Breakachie saw his priorities in a different light.

> 'I put no value upon you or your bairns unless you can bring me forth immediately thirty thousand men in arms ready to serve my master.'

Whereupon, he set off to return to Charles, taking John Roy Stewart with him. However, John Roy Stewart was informed only that he was going to meet Lochiel and other fugitives. He was not told about Charles.

The Prince

The Prince's companions: Donald MacDonnell of Loch Garry, Donald Cameron of Lochiel.

John MacPherson arrived at the Cage round about one o'clock in the morning. Despite the lateness of the hour, Charles insisted on beginning the journey to the coast immediately. Lochiel, who was now able to walk well enough, accompanied them. At Uisge Chaoil Reidhe, they rested throughout the day in the bothy they had used previously on the way to the Cage.

When a messenger arrived to warn Charles of the arrival of Young Breakachie and John Roy Stewart, Charles planned a surprise for John Roy Stewart. He wrapped himself up in a plaid, and lay on the floor. Just as John Roy Stewart entered the bothy, Charles peeped out. Whereupon, the astounded John Roy Stewart cried out, 'O Lord! My Master!', and fell into a puddle in a faint.

Loch Pattack

191

Young Breakachie had brought three fusees belonging to Charles. One fusee was mounted with gold, another with silver, and the third was half mounted. Charles was delighted to have them back.

'It is remarkable that my enemies have not discovered one farthing of my money, a rag of my cloathes, or one piece of my arms.'

In the evening, they set off again. The pace was slow because Lochiel could not walk quickly. Also, Charles was again suffering from 'looseness of flux'. In order to save time, they decided not to go via Meallan Odhar and the Corrieyairack Pass. Instead, they went via Loch Pattack straight to Glen Spean, which they crossed before stopping in Coir a Mhaigh at daybreak.

Loch a Bhealach Lean Bhan

27
14 - 20 SEPTEMBER
GLEN SPEAN to LOCH NAN UAMH

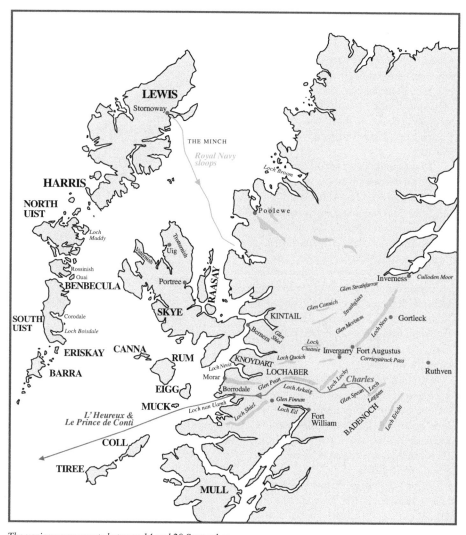

The various movements between 14 and 20 September

The Enemy

While the two French ships waited in Loch nan Uamh, there was an ideal opportunity for the Hanoverian forces to organise an ambush for Charles. However, neither the navy nor the army was patrolling the area.

All the Royal Navy's frigates were off the Orkneys, looking for the two privateers which, having deserted O'Sullivan in August, were now raiding merchant shipping. The only naval presence in the Minch was a small flotilla of sloops. Until 18 September, these ships were all in Stornoway harbour, sheltering from a gale. They then sailed for Gairloch.

Throughout this period, the presence of the two French ships was well known in the area. Several of Albemarle's informers sent messages to Stornoway and Fort Augustus for several days after the French ships had arrived. Amazingly, these messages took nearly two weeks to arrive. The news reached Stornoway on 18 September, but only after the sloops had left. It reached Lord Loudoun at Fort Augustus on 17 September. However, as Loch nan Uamh was some fifty miles distant, a sizeable force could not get there for some days.

How and why such a delay occurred is not known. It may be that those, who were responsible for transmitting the messages, were all conniving directly or indirectly with Charles' rescuers. Thus, Charles may have had some friends among his enemies.

At the same time, he had enemies among his friends. In particular, the Edinburgh tailor, Donald MacDonald, was 'well affected to His Majesty's Government', and 'did occasionally give Information to the Campbells'.

He had arrived in March to collect debts from his customers in Lochaber. For many months, he had been unable to leave due to ill-health. During his time by Loch nan Uamh, he had won the friendship and trust of the residents. It is surprising that he did not set out to inform the authorities immediately the two ships arrived. In fact, he did not leave until 16 September, but, instead of taking the news to Fort William, he set off towards Edinburgh. He was then delayed at Strontian, where a gang of Camerons robbed him, and held him captive for three days. Only after his release, did he report to the Deputy Governor of Fort William.

There was also an unknown Hanoverian mole who was a confidante of Charles' most trusted friends. Evidently, he had been in regular correspondence with Albemarle, but was unable to reveal his knowledge to the authorities in time to endanger Charles. A letter he wrote to Albemarle on 26 September reveals that he knew some closely guarded secrets.

'Since I was honoured with yours I did not chuse till now to give an account of what had passed at the meeting I had with Lochiel and Clunie, ... At that meeting it was consulted whether to provide a Ship immediately for carrying them off, or wait to see if the Pretender would make his appearance among them. I advised Lochiel to surrender himself to you, but the other opposed it, and then it was resolved that Lochiels brother and Lochgary should go in search of the Pretender, and were determined to find him out if in any part of the Main Land;

accordingly they go, and I come home, and soon as he was descovered they were to acquaint me of it; in six days thereafter I received a Letter from them giving account that he was found with six of Glenmorison's men whom he met accidentally in the Muir three or four days after he made his escape out of the Isle of Sky, and passing in the night time thro' the Centries that were posted at the head of Locharkeg, he travelled three days and two nights all alone, without meat or drink except water, and by accident met with those six men, with whom he continued for a month and some days, living upon flesh and water the whole time; when Lochgarry and the Doctor met him, he would fain persuade them to gather as many as they could and acquaint all their Friends to come to a Body in order to procure their peace or die sword in hand; this proposal was communicated to Lochiel and Clunie but they refused it, calling it a Don Quixote Scheme, and tho' they should be willing, that it was impossible to raise one man; and therefore they advised the Pretender to come and stay with them for his greater Security, and that they would endeavour to provide a ship in a short time. Accordingly he was prevailed upon to come to them about the 7th Inst, where he stayed to the 15th, when they were acquainted by Express from Clanranold that two 30 Gun ships arrived in Arisaig inquiring for him;'

The Friends

While they waited to hear from Charles, the two rescue ships stayed in Loch nan Uamh. The crews tried to give away the meal that they had confiscated from the *May*. However, the locals were reluctant to accept it. The Frenchmen also entertained local residents on board *Le Prince de Conti*.

As news of the ships' arrival travelled through the neighbourhood, some two hundred other fugitives visited the ships seeking escape or information. In particular, they included Young Clanranald and Barrisdale. Despite the fact that the locals suspected Barrisdale of treachery, they allowed him to leave to settle his affairs. However, they determined to arrest him on his return.

When the weather improved, the captains of the two French ships were worried about being discovered at anchor by the Royal Navy. On 15 September, they and the *May*, manned by a French crew, attempted to leave the loch for a patrol in the Minch, 'but the Wind soon coming contrary they came to Anchor'. The next day, they were more successful, and were able to cruise between Skye and Eigg, before returning safely to Loch nan Uamh in the evening.

The Prince

The Prince's companions: Donald MacDonnell of Loch Garry, Donald Cameron of Lochiel, Allan Cameron, Donald MacPherson of Breakachie, John Roy Stewart and four servants.

Exhausted after the night's journey, Charles and his friends slept throughout the morning deep in Coir a Mhaigh. Being a long way from any habitation, they felt safe enough to pass the latter part

Coir a Mhaigh

196

of the day with a shooting competition, in which they fired at bonnets thrown into the air. As a trained marksman, using his own fusees, 'his Royal Highness by far exceeded'.

In the evening, they set off walking, but, after only three or four miles, they rested for several hours by the Uisge nam Fichead. Charles' debilitating condition may well have been the reason. Later, they resumed the journey, and crossed the Roy before daylight. Then, they stopped and 'kept themselves private all day'. They stayed in the valley of Caol Lairig, where 'a trustye man', Murdoch MacPherson, kept a store of meal that Cluny had left for use on journeys between Badenoch and Achnacarry.

In the early hours of 16 September, they reached the River Lochy, which was so much in flood that it was impossible to wade. While debating how to overcome this obstacle, they were discovered by Cameron of Clunes. Having been alerted by Cluny and Archibald Cameron, Clunes had already been making preparations for Charles' arrival. When Lochiel enquired how they could get over, Clunes had the instant solution.

'Very well, for I have an old boat carried from Loch Arkaig that the enemy left unburnt of all the boats you had, Lochiel.'
Inspecting the vessel, Lochiel was full of doubt.

'I am afraid we will not be safe in it.'
Clunes, on the other hand, insisted that the boat was watertight. Furthermore, he was willing to prove it.

'I will cross first and show you the way,' he said.

He also knew how to make his friends more confident.

'I have six bottles of brandy, and I believe all of you will be the better of a dram.'

Lochiel, went to the Prince and said, 'Will your Royal Highness take a dram?'

'O,' said the Prince, 'Can you have a dram here?'

'Yes,' replied Lochiel, 'And that from Fort Augustus too.'

'Come, let us have it,' said Charles.

After drinking three of the bottles, they used the boat to cross the river in three precarious trips. Clunes led the first, and Charles the second. In the last, led by Lochiel, 'the crazy boat laked so much that there would be four or five pints of water in the bottom of the boat, and, in hurrying over, the three remaining bottles of brandy were all broke'.

With this unnerving experience behind him, Charles called for another dram. Sadly, he learned the news about the bottles, and was also informed that 'the common fellows had drunk all that was in the bottom of the boat as being good punch.' Thereafter, they were 'so merry that they made great diversion to the company as they marched along'. In the early hours of the morning, they arrived at Achnacarry, where they rested, and passed the whole of the next day.

During the night of 17 September, they walked along the south side of Loch Arkaig to Gleann Camgharaidh, where Cluny and Archibald Cameron, having completed their business with the gold, were waiting. They killed a cow, and ate the beef with bannocks made from meal that Cluny had brought with him from Caol Lairig. Thus, 'his royal highnes and his whole retinue were regalled and feasted plentifully that night'.

At this point, Charles wrote Cluny a letter reaffirming his promise to make good the losses that Cluny had suffered during the rebellion.

'As we are sensible of your and Clan's fidelity and integrity to us dureing our adventures in Scotland and England in the year 1745 and 1746, in recovering our just rights from the Elector of Hanover, by which you have sustained very great loss both in your interest and person, I therefore promise when it shall please God to put it in my power, to make a gretful return sutable to your suferings.'

(18 September, 1746)

Gleann Camgaraidh

Charles was concerned that the navy may soon discover the ships, if they had not already done so. He wanted to reach the ships as soon as possible. Being just twenty miles away, he decided to continue their journey in broad daylight, rather than wait for nightfall.

Along the way, the party accidentally met John MacHouvel, who happened to know Charles, Lochiel, Archibald Cameron and Lochgarry by sight. When they realised that MacHouvel had recognised them, they feared he

Loch Beoraid from the east

might inform the troops, before they arrived at the ships. They decided to make him accompany them, and to let him go only on arrival at Loch nan Uamh. This was a wise precaution, because MacHouvel informed the troops of the encounter within hours of his release.

Charles and his friends arrived at Loch nan Uamh late in the afternoon of 19 September. Charles took his leave of Cluny, Young Breakachie and the servants on the shore He was then taken on board *Le Prince de Conti* with Lochiel, Archibald Cameron, Lochgarry and John Roy Stewart. Later, they were all taken over to *L'Heureux*.

'About six in the Evening after sitting to Supper a Message came from the Conti, upon which Colonel Warren and the Captain of the Frigate got up in great hurry, got on their best clothes,'

There, Charles wrote final letters to be taken to those still at the shore.

'My lads, be in good spirits, it shall not be long before I shall be with you and shall endeavour to make up for the loss you have suffered. I have left money for your subsistence that are officers and have also left money to provide meal for all the private men.'

A letter to Cluny gave instructions on how this money was to be distributed. For the clansmen, £150 was to be given to Glengarry's, £300 to Lochiel's, £100 to each of the MacGregors and Stewarts. Charles also ordered payments of £100 to Lady Keppoch and to Cluny himself.

Over two hundred other Jacobite fugitives had collected at Loch nan Uamh, hoping to escape to France on the ships. For various reasons, Charles had some sixty of these put ashore. Those allowed to stay on board, included de Lancize and Berar.

'When they again saw the Prince and knew him to be such they were greatly ashamed that they had used him like a common man, in which shape he had formerly appeared to them.'

Two very reluctant passengers were Barrisdale and his son, who were arrested and put in irons, as soon as Charles embarked.

The final preparations included the disposal of the *May* and her crew. Since the *May* was not considered to be worth confiscating, they agreed to a request from her captain that his ship and crew be released for a ransom. Round about two in the morning, Warren boarded the *May t*o receive the payment of £180. As the captain of the *May* later reported,

> '[Warren] was in Top spirits and seemed greatly elevated with his extraordinary success telling me plainly he had now got the Prince, meaning the young Pretender, on board.'

With all the preparations complete, the two French ships set sail between two and three o'clock in the morning of 20 September. On board, 'the gentlemen, as well as the commons were seen to weep though they boasted of being soon back with an irresistible force'.

Over the previous ten weeks, Charles had trekked over the most gruelling countryside on the mainland. He was ill-equipped. He was ill. He was hungry. He had endured the most atrocious weather conditions. He was in constant danger.

> 'I shall only add that the Prince submitted with patience to his adverse fortune, was chearful, and frequently desired those that were with him to be so. He was cautious when he was in the greatest danger, never at a loss in resolving what to do, with uncommon fortitude.
> He regretted more the distress of those who suffered for adhering to his interest than the hardships and dangers he was hourly exposed to.
> To conlude, he possesses all the virtues that form the character of a HERO and GREAT PRINCE.'

Lochaber No More': A painting by John Blake MacDonald

200

The traditional site of Charles' departure

Index

Bibliography

ANG, T. & POLLARD, M., *Walking the Scottish Highlands: General Wade's Military Roads* (1984)

BARRON, E. M., *Prince Charlie's Pilot* (1913)

BLACK, J., *Culloden and the '45* (1990)

BLAIKIE, W. B., *Origins of the Forty-Five* (1916)

BLAIKIE, W. B., *Itinerary of Prince Charles Stuart from his landing in Scotland July 1745 to his departure in September, 1746* (1897)

CHAMBERS, R., *History of the Rebellion* (1869)

CHIDSEY, D. B., *Bonnie Prince Charlie* (1928)

DAICHES, D., *Charles Edward Stuart* (1973)

DOUGLAS, H., *Charles Edward Stuart, the Man, the King, the Legend* (1975)

DOUGLAS, H. *Flora MacDonald the Most Loyal Rebel* (1993)

DOUGLAS, H., *Bonnie Prince Charlie in Love: The Private Passions of Prince Charles Edward Stuart* (1995)

DUMONT-WILDEN, L., *The Wandering Prince* (1934)

ERICKSON, C., *Bonnie Prince Charlie* (1993)

EWALD, A. C., *The Life and Times of Prince Charles Stuart, Count of Albany.* (1904)

FERGUSSON, SIR JAMES, *Argyll in the '45* (1952)

FORSTER, M., *The Rash Adventurer* (1974)

FRANCIS, G. R., *The Romance of the White Rose* (1933)

GIBSON, J. S., *Ships of the '45. The Rescue of the Young Pretender* (1967)

GIBSON, J. S., *Lochiel of the '45* (1994)

GRAHAM, H. G., *The Social Life of Scotland in the Eighteenth Century* (1899)

GRANT, I. F., *Highland Folk Ways* (1961)

HADDEN, J. C., *Prince Charles Edward: His life, times and fight for the crown,* (1913)

HALDANE, A. R. B., *The Drove Roads of Scotland* (1952)

HARTMANN, C. H., *The Quest Forlorn* (1952)

HOME, J., *The History of the Rebellion 1745-46* (1802)

JOHNSTONE, CHEVALIER DE, *A Memoir of the 'Forty -Five* (1820)

LANG, A., *Prince Charles Edward Stuart* (1903)

LENMAN, B. P., *The Jacobite Risings in Britain, 1689 - 1746* (1980)

LENMAN, B. P., *The Jacobite Threat: A Source Book* (1990)

LINKLATER, E., *The Prince in the Heather*, (1965)

LIVINGSTONE, A., AIKMAN, C. W. H. & HART, B. S, *Muster Roll of Prince Charles Edward Stuart's Army, 1745 - 46* (1984)

MACDONALD, A., *Memorial of the '45* (1930)

MACDONALD, D. J., *Clan Donald* (1978)

MACDONALD, N. H., *The Clan Ranald of Knoydart and Glengarry* (1979)

MARSHALL, R. K., *Bonnie Prince Charlie* (1988)

MACLEAN, A., *A MacDonald for the Prince* (1982)

MACLEAN, A. & GIBSON, J. S., *Summer Hunting a Prince* (1992)

MACLEAN, SIR FITZROY, *Bonnie Prince Charlie* (1988)

MACLEOD, R. H., *Flora MacDonald* (1995)

McLAREN, M., *Bonnie Prince Charlie* (1972)

McLYNN, F. J., *France and the Jacobite Rising of 1745* (1981)

McLYNN, F. J., *The Jacobites* (1985)

McLYNN, F. J., *Charles Edward Stuart - A Tragedy in Many Acts*, (1988)

M'DONELL, J., *Spanish John*, (1931)

MURRAY OF BROUGHTON, J. (ed Bell, R. F.), *Memorials* (1898)

NICHOLAS, D., *The Young Adventurer: The Wanderings of Prince Charles Edward Stuart in Scotland in the Years 1745 - 46* (1949)

NORRIE, W. D., *The Life and Adventures of Prince Charles Edward Stuart*, 4 vols (1900)

PATTON, H. (ed), *The Lyon in Mourning*, 3 vols (Edinburgh, Scottish History Society, 1895)

PETRIE, SIR CHARLES, *The Jacobite Movement - The Last Phase* (1950)

PLANT, M., *The Domestic Life of Scotland in the 18th Century* (1952)

PORCELLI, BARON, *The White Cockade* (1949)

POWER, W., *Prince Charlie* (1912)

PRESTON, D., *The Road to Culloden Moor: Bonnie Prince Charlie and the '45 Rebellion* (1995)

STEWART, J., *The Camerons: A History of Clan Cameron* (1974)

TAYLER, A. & H., *1745 and After* (1938)

TAYLOR, W., *The Military Roads in Scotland* (1976)

TERRY, C. S., *Albemarle Papers* , 2 vols (Aberdeen, 1902)

TERRY, C. S., *The Rising of 1745* (1903)

TERRY, C. S., *The Life of the Young Pretender* (1903)

URE, J. A., *Bird on the Wing* (1992)

WILKINSON, C., *Bonnie Prince Charlie* (1932)

YOUNGSON, A. J., *The Prince and the Pretender* (1985)

Acknowledgements

All landscape photographs except one were taken by the author. The photograph on page 106 of the cave at Elgol was taken by Bob McMillan, who has kindly given permission for it to be used in this book.. The portraits and other illustrations have been provided by the following organisations holding the copyrights.

Aberdeen City Libraries
A highland settlement (p 16)

British Museum
Dr Archibald Cameron (p 166)

Caledonian Books
19th century maps (pp 137 and 162)

National Library of Scotland
Proclamations (pp 20 and 21)

National Maritime Museum, Greenwich
18th century frigate and sloop (pp 33 and 34)

National Portrait Gallery
Duke of Cumberland (p 23)
Lord Albemarle (p 132)
'Betty Burke' (p 83)
Flora MacDonald (p 72)

National Portrait Galley of Scotland
Highland dress (p 16)
Lord Loudoun (p 174)
Lady Margaret MacDonald (p 89)

Osprey Publishing
Hanoverian soldiers (p 23)

Ordnance Survey/OS data © Crown copyright 2015
Sketch maps in all chapters

Perth Museum and Art Gallery and Kinross Council
'Lochaber No More' (p 199)

Royal Bank of Scotland plc © 2015
General John Campbell (p 33)

Royal Collection Trust / © Her Majesty Queen Elizabeth II 2015
Prince Charles Edward Stuart (p 13)

Scottish History Society
Quotations from various publications

West Highland Museum Trustees of the West Highland Museum, Fort William
Cameron of Lochiel (p 166)

The author wishes to thank these organisations for their support and permissions to use their materials.